5.7-69

# THE
# BIRTH OF GOD

A Modern Priest Looks at His Outdated Church
*The Struggle of the Unbeliever*

# THE
# BIRTH OF GOD

*by*

*James Kavanaugh*

Trident Press
New York

SBN: 671-27018-4

LIBRARY OF CONGRESS CATALOG CARD NUMBER: 69-16054

COPYRIGHT, ©, 1969, BY JAMES KAVANAUGH

PUBLISHED SIMULTANEOUSLY IN THE

UNITED STATES AND CANADA BY TRIDENT PRESS,

A DIVISION OF SIMON & SCHUSTER, INC.,

630 FIFTH AVENUE, NEW YORK, N.Y. 10020.

PRINTED IN THE UNITED STATES OF AMERICA

1495267

## ACKNOWLEDGMENTS

With gratitude to my editor, Mr. Gene Prakapas, and to the friends who have encouraged me: Mr. Bill Reed, Mr. Bill Brockley; my brothers, Bob and Phil; my sister, Gail.

A special word of thanks to Bishop James A. Pike and Dr. Carl Rogers for their encouragement and inspiration.

A unique word to my wife, Pat, for her patience and understanding in turbulent times.

*To Pat*

# INTRODUCTION

It is difficult to view religion with any kind of perspective when one is emotionally involved with some particular sect or when one is struggling to extend the power of the religious institution. When I was a priest, people made it impossible for me to look objectively at the Church. They refused to relate to me except as Catholic priest, and this prevented them from telling me the truth and encouraged them to support my religious bias. Even when they disagreed with me, they were seldom direct and honest in their confrontation. They dismissed me with the traditional kind of tolerance that is offered to religious institutions and their leaders: "All religions are good." They were content to praise me for my dedication, to accept my sincerity, to respect my concern for men.

When I finally grew disillusioned enough by my own Catholic Church to write a critical book, *A Modern Priest Looks at His Outdated Church*, I was still anticipating the reform of my Church and hoped that my words would play some part in its renewal. Ordinary people, and even clergymen, responded well to what I said. Protestants and Jews, as well as Catholics, admitted that the sickness I wrote about existed in every religious institution. But my primary concern was with the Church I had known since childhood, the Church to which I had dedicated my life.

Since I have left the Church, I am now able to take an additional step and to look at the entire religious tradition of the Western World and its long-established mythology. I am able to recognize the privileged position that the religious institution has been given in our society, and the power it has had to color every kind of authority, not only religious, but social and political and parental as well. I now recognize that the religious phenomenon has affixed itself to our entire culture and has deprived man of the freedom that is his right and the maturity that is the hope of the world.

In this book I have attempted to reveal the origin of long-standing religious myths which have prevented man from being himself. I have reflected upon modern man, the man whom Marshall McLuhan has fittingly called "the man of the global village," the man who wears "all of mankind on his skin," and I have tried to describe his need to escape the slavery fashioned by superstition and sterile tradition. I believe that this modern man wants to be free from the religious institution, and I want to help him in his courageous struggle.

I recognize that such an undertaking is an ambitious one. With the help of an outstanding editor and close personal friends I have rewritten and rethought this book many times over. It has been a more difficult book to write than *A Modern Priest* because it did not flow as much from the intensity of my personal anguish as it did from quiet research and long reflection. But I consider it also a more important book because it attempts to go to the historical roots of the religious experience of the ordinary man. As before, I do not write to scholars, I write to men and women who are attempting to find love, to raise families, to live responsibly, to believe honestly, to attain personal freedom and maturity.

I am aware that this book will be offensive to some because religious myths take on a kind of "divine" significance. I welcome the criticism of all men because I am no longer attempting to defend the Church that I inherited but to discover the God Who gives meaning to my life. I expect to learn from my critics, not, of course, from their harsh and angry words, but from their own personal insights and reflections. I have no need in this book to say the "last word," only to say an honest one.

And regardless of critics, I know that millions of men are ready for what is written here. They want to be free from the religious mythology that has held them captive. They want to escape the religious institution that has attempted to determine man's goodness by its traditional categories and in the process has detracted from his own strength and put limits on his personal responsibility. They want to find their brother everywhere and not be impeded by the prejudice of the various religious traditions. It is for these men that I write, for the countless millions who are ready to be free and ultimately responsible for their own behavior.

A free man pays a terrible price for his freedom. No longer can he blame his society for its shortcomings, no longer can he anticipate "divine" deliverance from the inhumanity of man to man. He does not hide behind a hero, nor does he cower behind the elaborate rationalizations of a religious tradition. He must bear the burden of human pain himself, he must look to his own heart to understand evil, he must rely on his own mind and power to pursue peace and meaning in his own life. It is to the man who wants to be free that I write, the man who is prepared to be responsible for his own actions and the condition of his world. And in the free and responsible behavior of such a man is the genuine *birth of God*.

It is hard for me to believe the changes that have taken place in my life during the past two years. I have left the Catholic priesthood, I have left the institutional Church, and I have married. Actually I have changed my whole way of life. Three years ago I did not anticipate any of this. I was disappointed with the Church, disillusioned by the action of the bishops after Vatican II, and filled with indignation at the refusal of my Church to face reality. When I toured the country to discuss *A Modern Priest*, I became aware of the great religious unrest in society. I learned that my own religious transformation had only begun. I discovered, as I read and entered into discussions with other sincere men, and as I spent countless hours in reflection, that my religious position was not a static one. I had more growing to do.

Gradually I realized that I was not a Catholic, that I did not want to be, and that I wanted the record cleared. I felt some responsibility to the people who had read and approved the story of *A Modern Priest*. When they wrote to me, or when they spoke with me, they expected me to be the same man I was when I took leave of the priesthood. This book is also an attempt to tell the people who gained courage from my ideas where I have gone since I wrote my first book. I am not sure that all will be pleased by my personal development. I anticipate that I will receive rejection and condemnation from some of them. I would not be honest if I were to say that this makes no difference. I am a sensitive person and harsh words hurt me, but they will not prevent me from writing what I believe to be true.

I wrote this book to be honest, because I did not want to

appear as something I am not. I wrote it because I am convinced that millions of men are at the same stage of religious development as I am, and that they will profit from what I have to say. I wrote it in the hope that they will not have to suffer the guilt and anguish that I have suffered in attempting to escape the fierce hold of the religious institution. I wrote it in the hope that parents who have lived honestly and successfully within the religious institution, who have raised their families by its codes and doctrines, will better understand that their children are not rejecting them when they reject the Church. I wrote it to offer some leadership for the young whose faith will never be satisfied by the narrow goals of the Church. I wrote it because I felt qualified to write it, because only a man who has taken the Church as seriously as I have in the past can know the power of its grasp on men.

Millions of men have turned away from the churches; millions more will follow as they discover how exhilarating it is to be a free man. But they will often suffer when they leave the Church, not merely because their families and friends will judge them harshly, not merely because they will feel cut off from their childhood, but most of all because they will feel a responsibility to do something about the plight of helpless men. They will be a part of the whole world, a brother to every man, a part of every injustice that makes man a prisoner.

Once as a priest I could demand man's obedience by the power of my office. I could force his compliance by the fury of my threats of punishment. Now I can only talk to him, offer my friendship, try to open up my heart. Now I feel as feeble as he does. And in this common feebleness, I sense our concerted strength. In our common struggle, I experience the *birth of God.*

# CONTENTS

# THE
# BIRTH OF GOD

# 1. THE SEARCH

It was June, 1966, the twelfth anniversary of my ordination to the priesthood. I backed out of the driveway of my parents' home in Michigan; I had said "good-bye" to them even though they did not understand the reason for my journey. My mother stood in the doorway and cried openly. My dad was flushed and upset. I wanted to get out of the car and tell them I loved them, but I knew I had to go. I left in a little blue Volkswagen filled with everything I owned. My destination was my brother's home in California. I had five hundred dollars to my name.

The day before, I had talked to my bishop and had tried to tell him why I wanted to take a leave of absence from the priesthood. He did not understand. He asked me to remain and be a pastor in a parish. But I couldn't. So he reluctantly gave me a leave of absence and I left to go to California. There I was to write a book about why I found it difficult to be a priest. My bishop would read it and not understand. Nor would my parents, although I know they love me.

I arrived in San Diego after stopping briefly in Mexico. I had planned to stay in Mexico to brush up on my Spanish. I took up residence with a family in Morelia. They offered me room and board for sixty dollars a month. But the book gnawed at me and I only stayed a week. I tried to tell the family in faltering Spanish that I had not been disappointed with my accommodations. I just had to leave and write, but they did not understand.

In San Diego, I took an apartment. It was a strange sensation since I never had an apartment of my own. I bought some food and dishes, a cookbook, a few sheets and towels, and dug in to write a book. I met some of my neighbors but only gradually dared to tell them that I was a priest. When I told them, it didn't seem to matter. That surprised me. I had thought that they wouldn't speak to me, or that they would condemn me. But no one seemed concerned or even especially interested.

When I finished the book, I took a job in a counseling institute. I was more fortunate than most priests who leave. My brother was director of the institute. He offered me the job. Looking back, it was wrong of me to lean on him, but I was afraid and did not know what else to do. Shortly after I came to the institute, we stopped receiving referrals from Catholic parishes. My brother was not considered a good enough Catholic. He did not go to church and he now harbored an "ex-priest." My presence in the institute undoubtedly cost him a lot of money, but in his characteristic way he said, "The hell with it." But now I know I should have stood on my own feet. I had never learned such independence in the priesthood.

About the time I came to the institute I met the girl who would become my wife. I liked her the minute I met her at a friend's apartment. We only talked a few minutes that night. When she asked what kind of work I did, I was afraid to tell her that I was a priest on leave. I told her on our first real date, and it didn't seem to trouble her. She was not a Catholic and had never really known a priest, but she seemed to like me.

Working at the institute was difficult. I was self-conscious and worried about what people might think of me. My clients didn't seem to care about my past; they were in search of understanding and help. Through those early months at the institute, I still thought about remaining in the priesthood. But I did not know what I wanted. I was lonely and confused and my mind was in constant turmoil. I had known nothing but the Church since I was a little boy.

I had gone to the seminary when I was fifteen and had worked hard. I received praise for my efforts and was told I would make a good priest. I was ordained in 1954 and was sent to the cathedral parish in Lansing, Michigan. It was the first of three assignments. For a time, I worked among the Mexican migrants and I enjoyed it. Later, I would have a chance to work among the Negroes. This was work that had interested me, since I had served as a director of a Negro playground a few years before I became a priest. But most of the time I worked among the middle class, people whose attitudes and background were similar to my own. I worked with college students and taught in high school. I was lonely, but I seemed to have no doubts about the teaching of the Church. Or if I had doubts, I repressed them.

In the summer of 1963, I returned to school to earn a degree in theology, or more properly, religious philosophy. I was still narrow and unswerving in my loyalty to the Pope and to the Church. When the birth control problem was discussed, I was violent in my defense of the Church's position. I could not think for myself; the consequences were too great. I could not endanger my faith. While I was at the university, the Catholic University in Washington, D.C.,

Vatican II was taking place. The discussions about the council began to open my eyes. I began to ask questions that had always been vaguely at the back of my mind. In the confessional and in private discussions with my friends, I began to admit the doubts that came to me. I became associated with the more liberal of the graduate students. I read everything I could get my hands on which explored the doctrines and moral teachings of my Church. My doubts increased.

I went to Europe in the summer of 1964 to attend the lectures of the great theological minds of England, Germany, and France. This was an important period in my life. I met personally the men whose books I had read, and I asked them the questions that had gone unanswered in their treatises. I was unhappy with their answers; they did not seem to understand the real problems of our time. They were serious and sincere scholars who seemed to know little about men. They were not able to help me.

One of my associates that summer was a professor of sociology at a small college in Alabama. He was Jewish, but more important, he was human and of considerable help to me. He helped me to understand that I could not look to other men for answers that I must provide myself. He said that scholarship could not help me now, only courage. We often talked far into the night, and up to that point in my life, I had never met such an open and honest man. He helped me to believe in myself. He helped me to overcome the handicap of my priestly education that had forced me to base any personal opinion on some ancient authority.

I returned to the university in the fall and my confusion grew. I found it difficult to hear confessions and to say Mass. Yet I went through the motions and tried desperately to be a priest. I said Mass at a girls' college near the university, and the students seemed to sense my struggle. I gave their retreat and refused to cater to the theological traditions of the Catholic Church. Rumors spread, questions were asked, several priests attacked my "liberalism."

Somehow, when I reached San Diego, all this was past. I had taken off my collar and had begun wearing a tie. Then the book which I had written several months before was featured in *Look*, and my life was no longer quiet. I was asked to appear on television, to be interviewed by the press. For weeks, I did not have a minute to myself. My religious struggle was shared with millions of people. I was still battling with my own problems of faith, and I was asked to pass judgment on the feelings of thousands of other men.

I had been trying to learn to be a good counselor. I had been trying to understand my own feelings about the priesthood and the Church. I had been trying to get to know the woman who would later become my wife. I had been trying to learn to live as a layman. Suddenly I was in the midst of a giant struggle. Mail poured in and phone calls came from all over America and Canada. I had not been fully aware of the kind of book I had written. I had only wanted to tell my bishop and the friends who had trusted me, indeed to tell myself, why I found it difficult to be a priest. I had thought that some others would be interested, but I did not know the extent of the religious confusion in the world.

My friends realized that I was under tremendous pressure. It was not television that bothered me, though at times I was a little nervous. I did not mind the reporters or the antagonists who felt compelled to "take me on." I was struggling with my own conscience and the faith of my childhood. I did not know the future of the Church. I did not know the future of my own life. I only knew that I was struggling to find meaning and peace myself, and the questions asked by thousands of people obliged me to examine and reexamine my convictions. The struggle was not with my interrogators, but with my own heart and mind.

The Catholic press began to scream at me. They simplified my struggle and said that I was in "search of sex" or that I had "lost my faith." They called me "traitor," "theological imbecile," "money hungry," or "publicity hound." Their words hurt me deeply. I did not feel like any of the things they called me. I was tired, frightened, worried about my parents, wondering about my priesthood, struggling to keep up with my work. I had pondered for months over the contents of my book. I had weighed the words, felt each feeling at the core of my being, and longed to find my God. I was restless in my job, unsure in my romance, and fearful of the new responsibility that was mine. I wanted to run, but something inside of me would not let me. No one seemed to understand what I was about. Some called me "courageous" when I was only trying to find meaning in my life. Others called me "insane" when I asked questions that no one seemed to answer.

In August of 1967, I had started on the last leg of a television tour. I had broken up with my future wife and had told her that I was confused about my future. I loved her, I needed her, but I could not have her amid the struggle in which I was engaged. I made the appearances that were expected of me. I appeared on the *Today* show in August, and shortly after my interview I returned home. I was determined to make no more public appearances until I had taken stock of myself.

I spent hours in solitude, rethought my position, and asked

myself a thousand more questions than any interviewer had posed. I walked on the beach, read a bit, occasionally went to Mass.

Suddenly I realized that I had already given up on the institutional church. It was then that a huge weight was lifted from my shoulders. I resolved never to wear the collar again. I could no longer be a priest. I started dating my future wife again, although by this time she was ready to give me up for lost. I was still struggling, I still did not have the answers I needed about life's meaning, but I was asking nothing from the institutional church. I was on my own and I began to feel like a human being after what seemed like a hundred years of trying.

I thought of my summers at home during the seminary days. I remembered walking by the shore of the lake where we lived. I remembered how I prayed, how I begged God to make me feel worthwhile, how I pleaded with Him to give me the strength to go on and be a priest. No one knew me then, I hid from everyone, although I appeared friendly and at peace. I was in the midst of a lifelong turmoil, struggling to be free from sin, struggling to be dedicated to the service of men, struggling to find God.

But I now realized that I had never found Him in all the years of trying. I only found a historic church filled with ritual, dogmas, moral laws, and unyielding legalism. I found a church that would not change, a church that was laden with structures that had lost their meaning. I found mighty schools, a strong hierarchy, loyal people, endless traditions, and frightened members. But this was not enough. I wanted God.

In October of 1967, I was invited to speak at Notre Dame University. It was then that I formally announced my resignation from the priesthood, though I had not intended to at the time. As I talked to the students about the Church, its narrowness, its injustice, its superficial changes, and its lack of genuine contact with men, I saw the honest openness of the young faces about me. I had already told myself that I could no longer be a priest, and as I talked, I knew I had to tell the students. So I told them—in tears. I told them with the fury of emotions that had been buried for a lifetime.

A month later, I knew I was ready for marriage. I loved Pat very much, although the on-again, off-again status of our romance had nearly driven her mad. I wrote to the bishop and asked for permission to be married in the Church. It was not an honest thing to do. When I had resigned from the priesthood at Notre Dame, I had also left the institutional church. I really did not care to be married in the Church, but I thought it would make it easier for my parents to accept my marriage. But I was wrong. It is next to impossible for the parents of a former priest to understand. There is too much confusion and hurt. But I corresponded with my bishop several times. When he told me to delay my marriage, I refused, and Pat and I were married by an Episcopal priest in December of 1967. The local clergy were incensed, the local bishop was angry and almost rude, but I was happy and fulfilled.

I am still happy—not because life is easier, but because it is honest. I am no longer committed to any system of thought. I am no longer the slave of any traditional philosophy. My life is not a preplanned program, not a dedication to an ideal that men have forced upon me, but the excitement and pain of an honest search. I am not looking for the ultimate truth, I just want enough meaning to get me through the day. This is not always easy. Sometimes I wake up early in the morning or lie awake at night and wonder what it all means.

One evening my wife and I gave a party for a few friends. Some of the people had never met. It was a quiet party— more realistically—it was a disappointment. Afterward we were both depressed. The next day we were alone. We talked quietly about our deepest feelings and admitted the depths of our loneliness, the feebleness of our human love. We hid nothing, we were a trifle sad, we accepted the uncertainty of our lives. It was a sacred moment that we shared. We did not demand answers, we did not demand ecstatic joy. We reached out our hands in trust and beginning love. We did not know certainty, only a quiet kind of peace. We did not know God, only a gentle kind of meaning. We did not know an overpowering strength, only a fragile kind of hope.

Since leaving the Church, like every other man, I am lonely. But I can be honest, genuine, legitimate, real. I want to be loved, to feel the power of love, to be able to reach out and ask for another's hand, to admit my fear, my loneliness, my anger, my confusion, my joy, my peace. I do not feel stronger than another man, nor weaker. I do not compare myself to anyone. And yet, I can share the experience of another man and liken it to my own. I can reveal my weakness to another and know that it is similar to his. I can be myself and know that I am able to be loved.

I can better understand why many men are not able to leave the Church. It is not an easy way. The Church gives man something to lean on other than himself. It permits him to escape the deep questions that tear at the heart of a man who faces life as it is. The man in the institution does not have to know the anguish of the man who must say; "Does life mean anything?" He does not know the pain of a man

who says; "Why live at all?" But neither does he know the
faith of such a man, a blind and feeble faith, not in a system
but in the opaqueness of life and God. He does not know
the hope of such a man, not in a cultural myth with all of its
bold certainty but in the quiet uncertainty of every day, in
the tiny spark of honest love.

I will always remember the past with a kind of nostalgia. I
sometimes lie on the beach and hum the Gregorian chants
that I once sang in the seminary, the Kyrie with its solemn
dignity, the psalms with their melancholic strain. I think of a
little boy who recited his catechism and gave up candy
during Lent. I think of a seminarian who served a quiet Mass
in a crypt chapel and spent hours in a dark church on his
knees. I think of Christmas and Easter and the old church
where I believed as a schoolboy.

But such thoughts are little different from ones I have of
the woods I walked in, searching for rabbits and frogs. Nor
are they different from the memories I have of football
games on Sunday afternoons with the boys in my neighborhood, or of Halloween parties when we got sick on cider or
laughed till our sides ached. I feel nostalgia about my
brothers when they were little boys, about my parents when
they watched us gulp down mashed potatoes and the Sunday
roast, about my friends when we had no wrinkles or cares.

But I cannot go back. Neither the Church nor the family
life of my childhood can be restored. Neither is anything
more than a memory. Now, I must live with the realities of
today.

I have not given up my religion, I have only matured.
Once I knelt before a statue of the Virgin Mary and poured
out my heart. Now I am able to tell my wife that I love her
and know that love is not the poetic affection I gave to Mary.

Once I paid homage to the mystery of God by honoring Him in Trinity. Now I can feel the mystery of God's presence in men and know the pain of uncertainty, of blind and doubtful faith. Once I needed hell to tell me of man's suffering, of his inhumanity to other men. Now I can feel the terror of human suffering, the horror of a life without love, the anguish of human loneliness. Once I needed heaven to encourage me, to give me strength. Now I can face death with the little bit of meaning that I draw from every day. I know that each dogma I accepted from the Church is a partial truth which, when purged of its mythology, can have contemporary meaning. I know that each moral teaching, when purified and made human, contains a beautiful ideal. I do not mock these truths; I treasure them as the door to freedom which lies beyond them. Mythology has ever been the comfortable avenue to the more painful truth.

To some, it may seem that I have changed quickly. In a way, they are right. Once the door of my mind was opened, once I saw how completely I had leaned on the Church and its well-meaning myths, once I saw how I had been tied to my family and my fears, I was able to abandon my childhood and to become a man. Then it was easy to see beyond sin and hell, sacrament and salvation. But the first step toward openness, the first effort to pry open my mind and to face my fears seemed to take a thousand years. I feel that I have fought beside every pilgrim who said his rosary on the way to a roadside shrine, that I have struggled beside every bishop whose mitre I respected, whose ring I kissed. I have battled beside every priest who forgave my sins in kindness, beside every nun who told me of angels and the Devil's wrath. I have relived every memory of a mother who taught me to pray and who let me put the infant in the Christmas crib.

And I cannot forget. I can only weep and continue to search in the joyful agony of a new freedom, in the pain of standing before God on my own. To be thus is not to "lose one's faith." It is for the first time in life really to have faith. It is to be stripped of props and religious fantasies. It is to face the ultimate fear, the fear that life means nothing, and to live with it. It is to be a part of all the unrest that currently questions every traditional value in our society. It is to live with oneself, to learn one's own value, to abandon the religious myths of childhood, to grow mature enough to have faith.

Recently I had an important counseling experience with a father and his nineteen-year-old son. The father explained to me that his son was a failure at almost everything he tried to do. He had flunked out of college his second year. He had dated a girl who did not meet with the approval of the family. He had passed up a career in baseball because he got tired of practicing. He had very few friends, was unable to converse with people in the neighborhood, and spent far too much of his time in protesting the draft and marching for civil rights. The father admitted that his son had a right to different attitudes about society than his parents, but he insisted that the young man was not realistic about making a living. He was learning to be a mechanic when he had the talent and abilities to be a professional man.

The son spoke quietly and seemed hurt that he had disappointed his father. He said that he had never wanted to go to college, but had agreed to try it when his parents applied pressure. He said that the girl he had dated was quiet and shy and his parents only seemed to approve the college cheerleader type. He admitted that the "all-American girl" made him uncomfortable and self-conscious. His girl friend, on the other hand, had a quiet kind of honesty that he loved. He also talked about his work and spoke of it with pride. He said that he was becoming a good mechanic and that the job fascinated him. He admitted that he might get tired of it, but he wanted to find out for himself.

As the discussion continued, the feelings of the father and the son grew more intense. The father felt that the son was purposely disappointing him in some kind of adolescent rebellion. He spoke of his own life, how hard he had worked, how many sacrifices he had made for his son's happiness and education. The young man tried to explain, but the father did not seem to be able to listen. Finally the son's eyes filled with tears, his face was flushed and frightened, and he looked right at his father and said, "Dad, I'm trying to tell you who I am. I know you're disappointed. But can't you love me for what I am?"

That night, in the tension of their struggle, I saw the struggle of the world, the struggle of my own life. I saw a son asking his father: "If I am really myself, will you love me? If I throw away my masks, if I stop hiding what I feel, if I am weak and unsure, will you not reject me and demand that I be strong and successful and confident? If I am honest, can I not be your son?" I saw man begging his fellowman: "Please love me for what I am."

This is what I once asked the Church and it refused. So I left the Church. And I have discovered that I do not need its certainties. I can live with uncertainty. I can take any position that seems honest. And I can change that position when new evidence or experience demands it. I live with wonder, with mystery, and in the midst of doubts which are the very condition of life. That is not to say that I do not know anything; it is merely to say that I do not know everything. And in my uncertainty I have had to leave the certainty of the Church, and in doing this I have rediscovered my fraternity with men. I have stopped asking the Church to accept me, to approve my behavior or my faith. I have begun to accept myself, to abandon my myths, and, in this acceptance and freedom, to discover the birth of God.

A few months ago a priest visited me in my office. He was kind and concerned. He told me that I was doing a great deal of harm to simple and unsuspecting men. He said that I should not take the Church away from people until I had something to put in its place. This priest was willing to admit that much of religion is mere custom and even superstition, that much of faith is myth. He did not believe in the Trinity, or in purgatory, or in hell. He had doubts about the sacraments and the Mass. But he did not want to betray people and leave them helpless in the face of life.

I told him that I had more confidence in man. I said that I did not believe that something untrue would ultimately help anyone. He said that the Church needed more time, that the Pope and the bishops did not know where to turn. He pleaded with me to be patient. I liked him. He was a sincere man. But I did not like what he was saying. Systems of thought do not replace systems of thought like new buildings replace old ones. Change comes gradually, almost imperceptibly, but when most of us recognize it, it is already upon us.

He asked me what I had to put in the place of the Church. I told him that I had bits and pieces, only a beginning, only the courage to search, the faith to face uncertainty as a man and not as a child. I said I believed that man will find his own system, his own religion, if we tear down the idols that have kept him in slavery. The priest looked very sad when he told me that if the institution disappears, we will lose the values that we knew as children, there will be fear and confusion, authority will be undermined, sexual freedom will tear apart marriages and destroy young lives. He insisted that man will have no clear picture of the afterlife and will lose his reverence for God. He felt that religious traditions would pass away, that religious truths will be watered down or abandoned. He foresaw terror and savagery in the streets, misery and hostility in the homes, tears and hopelessness in human hearts. He asked finally, "What will be left?"

He will be left and so will I, so will the simple and hard-working, so will human love, and so will God. There will not be an end to authority, but a new authority based on honesty and not on superstition. There will be a genuine and fulfill-ing sexuality, not a preoccupation and prudishness nourished in the immaturity of the past. There will be an honest con-frontation with death, not the morbidity and terror that have made of man a coward and a slave. There will be man, ever yearning, ever searching, ever changing, ever growing.

As I write I watch the sun slowly push away the fog. I watch the water wash against the rocks. I watch the birds in the wind. And I know that I am of the world of fog and rocks and flying birds. I am man, the prince of the world, its pride and majestic monument. And in my being I feel the water and the sun, the joy of the sea gull and the quiet calm of the fog. I feel the ages gone and the ages ahead. I feel the victory of battles won and the challenge of battles yet to be fought. I feel in my bones the struggle of the animal to rise up and walk. In my blood I feel the heat of a thousand dead rebels and the passion of a thousand loves. In my heart I feel the joy and sadness of a thousand hearts who helped in the creation of mine.

But most of all I feel confidence and hope and the pain of the search. I do not need certainty. I do not need absolutes. I do not need unyielding structures or infallible teachers, because I am man and man can live with questions. I need to be loved; I am loved, and in this experience, I can search for a greater share of truth and a greater understanding of myself. But I need to be loved as I am, not as I could be, or might be. I need love now, and without tasting it, I can only live in meaningless agony and vain competition, in empty ambition and pointless pain, in utter loneliness and coldness, in childish devotion to the religious myths of my past. And to live thus is to be dead.

Once I was a priest and I was dead. Now I am a man and I am alive. I know that I count to someone, that it really makes a difference if I live or die. I know that my words, my touch, my pain are important. I know that I am priceless to another as weak and human as I am. And in this knowledge I have ceased struggling and have begun more calmly to search. I do not regret my years in the priesthood. Perhaps they make me better able to appreciate what I have. Now I do not live in fantasy, or blame myself for what God has built within my heart: the longing to be loved as I am. Now I do not "save" anyone, or try to "save" myself. I search for meaning and do the best I can.

I have no system, only a few ideas. I have no church, only a few friends. I have no ritual, only an embrace, a handshake, a quiet conversation. I have no vestments, only hands and heart and mind, a smile, a laugh, a tear. I have no master plan for the religious reconstruction of the world, only a boundless confidence that the man who abandons his religious myths and is free from his idols will discover God in the growing honesty and freedom of his own life. I am searching now, not struggling, and in this search and in the search of millions of other men, I sense the *birth of God*.

# 2. THE MAN
# OF THE "GLOBAL VILLAGE"

I was stunned one night while listening to the news. The commentator announced that a priest friend of mine had been excommunicated for marrying without the permission of the Church. I found it hard to believe that in the age of space technology a religious body could be so out of touch as to believe that such a mythological penalty could have any meaning left for man. (To excommunicate means to cut off a person from union with the Church.) This particular priest had served well as a pastor and as an educator within the system. He decided for his own reasons of conscience that he must live within the framework of marriage. He asked permission to leave honorably and was told that a petition would be sent to Rome. He waited for more than a year and then decided to ignore the Roman authority. He took a worthwhile job to support his wife and her children. The marriage took place and he settled down to the responsibilities of his new life. Then after a few months came the startling and public news that he was excommunicated.

Actually, even within the framework of the Church's own law, such an excommunication is invalid. There can be no excommunication unless it involves serious "sin" on the part of the subject who is punished in this way. The most any

Church authority could say is that this man incurred excommunication by marrying, if in so doing he had acted contrary to his own conscience. In this case the religious authority made no such qualification. A man had peered into the soul of another man and found him guilty. This is authoritarian arrogance of the most unpardonable kind.

Excommunication has been authority's way of playing God. It has been the inhuman and unchristian denial of man's freedom of conscience. But most of all it has been a frightened authority's frantic effort to dominate and control man rather than to direct him toward mature love. Excommunication attempts to turn the religious experience into a boot camp where the officer in charge aspires to build men by smothering them with confinement and indignity. Perhaps such methods have meaning in preparing a man for combat. They are only childish and dishonest in dealing with man's relationship with God.

Excommunication has its origin in another culture, when men saw portents in thunderstorms and evil omens in the flow of a chicken's blood. It is the product of an age when men could think of investing a king with divine prerogatives and dividing persons into rigid social classes. These were days when the rights of man were few, when the wealthy could live off the poor without any social protest, when Popes and bishops had the outlook and accoutrement of lords. But although these days are long gone, their decayed remains are still present enough to invade the television news and speak of excommunication.

Such exaggerated authority could flourish in a divided and fragmented world where man was isolated from his fellowman. It was a world in which a man could consider his own culture unique and special. The Frenchman could consider the German obese and stupid and could call him an aesthetic illiterate. The German could despise the Jew who was as much a German as he was and vow to exterminate him because his blood was not "Aryan." It was a world in which the American could mock the passion of the Italian and think that his children were all budding members of the Mafia. It was a world in which the Negro was a white man's valet and housemaid, and his mental capacity was said to be limited by his inferior protoplasm. It was a world in which the American thought the Japanese were cowardly and deceitful, that the Chinese were cruel and diabolically cunning. It was a world in which a man was taught to see his own family as deserving of lifelong loyalty no matter how fiercely it held him a prisoner and fostered bigotry and guilt. It was a world in which a religious sect could call itself infallible and absolute.  **1495267**

In such a world censorship—just like excommunication—was the accepted principle of survival, and isolation was the very condition of flourishing life. It was not merely the censorship and isolation demanded by the Catholic *Index of Forbidden Books,* but that created by man's inability to read any language but his own. Or that created by an educational administration which selected its own books and tailored its own courses. Or that created in a culture where the world of the East was a mystery to the man of the West. The very philosophy of education, limited as it was by its devotion to the printed word and to the "logical" development of ideas, by its programs of degrees and its required courses, by its teaching methods and the nature of its standardized exams, locked man in the narrowness of his own culture.

It was a world of walls, not merely the dramatic ones in Berlin and in Eastern Europe, not merely the tense one of

the Mandelbaum Gate dividing the Arab from the Jew, but
the wall in South America that divided the rich from the
poor, the wall in Canada that separated the French and the
English, the wall in America that held back the Polish
immigrant and accepted the Irish, the wall that kept the Jew
from country clubs and Negroes from the suburbs. It was the
wall that kept the African loyal to his colonial landlords, that
kept the Communist pouring out his propaganda, that kept
the United States supervising the various revolutions of the
world.

But now a new man is here, the product of an electronic
age. He is a man to whom boundaries mean nothing, for he
has conquered time and space. Marshall McLuhan writes
well of him, describing the "imperceptible alteration"
whereby he has been suddenly transformed and the "global
village" in which he now lives. No longer can he be remote,
no longer can he be out of touch; each man wears "all
mankind as [his] skin." The new "medium" of contact in
the world, the electronic medium, has a new "message":
*instantaneous communication*. A revolt in Peru or Bolivia is
heard and understood in Munich and Liverpool and Niles,
Michigan. An American war in Vietnam is protested in London and Berlin, in Paris and San Francisco. A student riot at
Berkeley or Columbia is reenacted in Budapest or at the
Sorbonne.

The new man does not have to run to the giant cities to be
a part of the world. The cities come to him in the remote-
ness of his own village, in the quiet privacy of his country
estate. Man is being made "emotionally aware of his total
interdependence with the rest of society." Once he relied on
the wheel to take him to distant cities, or he depended on
books to reveal to him foreign cultures. Now he can fly to

lands which were once a mystery, or he can remain at home and have these lands and their people brought to him. Even now he can hear instant translations of foreign tongues and talk of the day when there will be a universal language on the face of the earth. He can watch Olympic Games in Mexico, golf matches in Georgia, prizefights in Germany, murders in Memphis and Dallas. Once he read about men and women who wore strange clothes and ate exotic foods. Now he can communicate with these same men and women who dress much as he does; he can taste their recipes, enjoy their movies, share their art, study their politics, hear their leaders, dance to their music. He is the man of the "global village," where anywhere is soon to be everywhere.

Even now he travels from New York to California and has to remind himself where he is. He watches accents disappear, customs merge, differences dissolve. Once he would show slides when he went to Europe or drop hints about his travels around the world. Now millions are able to spend a vacation or further their education in foreign lands, while millions more find such travel routine and uninspiring. A man in San Diego is not a stranger in Paris, nor is a man in Seattle awed by the excitement of New York. Men everywhere are becoming a part of the global village which makes each city self-sufficient and in touch with the rest of the world.

Once, in the primitive village, man shared a closeness with every member of his tribe. There were, of course, quarrels and violence, anger and disagreements, but each man was comfortable in the security of his village. He knew its language, understood its customs, was familiar with its traditions. Nothing in the village was strange to him. The men around him were of the same color. There were differences in personality and talent, differences in courage and beauty and health. But the differences were nothing when compared with the common bond which united him to each member of his own tribe.

Now the world is becoming such a village, a global village beyond all boundaries. And the bond which unites its members is more than language or color or custom—for these are only artificial bonds. It is man united with man precisely because he shares a common manhood. No trivial difference can unsettle this essential bond of agreement. Differences are recognized, but they are of no great moment or consequence. Man is not afraid of differences. To be an American does not contain for me the emotion that once it did, the emotion that could move me to murder the Vietcong and to build the Communist into an unfeeling monster, the emotion that could urge me to hold myself apart from the rest of men. I am not passionately an American, I am passionately a man. I share something with Americans, indeed, but I share something far more important with *every* man.

In the global village, political differences are not of great import. To be a Republican or Democrat is merely to share a political leaning; it is no longer to embrace a unique way of life. And religious sectarianism only plays a superficial part. To be Catholic or Protestant or Jewish is only to describe an accident of birth or circumstances; it is only to admit one's past training. Such a commitment, no matter how deep and unyielding it seems, is only on the surface when compared with the depths of what man shares with man—because he is man.

Thus to the man of the global village, religious councils and conferences and ecumenical debates seem hardly worthy of intense concern. The enthusiasm of political conventions seems childish and unreal. The nationalistic pride that flows from the mouths of presidents and premiers seems archaic and ignorant. The man of the global village is at home everywhere, nothing is foreign to him, nothing is occult or esoteric. Every man, regardless of the superficial differences which will always mark human beings, can be the brother of every other man. Man, the member of the global village, is a citizen of the world, a world beyond sect and nation.

Such a world does not pride itself on the size of its factories or on the strength of its armies, on the variety of its consumer goods or on the amount of its gross national product. It is rather a world that is proud of the freedom and peace of its inhabitants, a world that despises the system that permits rich men to select their food lavishly while poor men are starving and out of work. It is a world that does not permit men to be denied the dignity that is their due, not as Americans or WASPs, not as aristocrats or whites, not as socialites or *litterati*, but as men. It will revolt in the face of such inequality and overthrow governments; it will take up arms and burn draft cards, boycott graduations and march on Washington. It is a new world in which man knows that he can be the brother of every other man, that the hatred and bigotry born of separation will be dissipated, that the inequality born of distance and ignorance will be dissolved. It is a world in which man recognizes how much he has in common with other men rather than how different he is.

Computers will run this new man's machines and free him to be a man. Wisdom will direct his schools and permit him to understand his world. Justice will direct his life and enable him to enjoy the only life he has. No president will stop him by shouting and blustering, no policeman will stop him by guns or snarling dogs, no politician will stop him by idle promises, no Pope will stop him by token reforms and archaic excommunications.

Such exaggerated authority still exists in some families. Parents insist that their daughter double-date until she is eighteen; they force a son to go to college, or demand that the family spend a vacation together no matter the ages and interests of their children. And if the youngster gets in some kind of trouble, suddenly they decide to play truant officer and private detective. These are the parents who cannot let go, who once disappointed cannot trust, who believe that freedom is a commodity suddenly purchased when a child leaves the family home. Sooner or later they are forced to make a choice. Either they must compromise and leave the maturing boy or girl the necessary freedom to make mistakes, or they must create some kind of physical or emotional imprisonment.

The Church and the temple have been such a dogmatic and controlling parent. So has my own government. So has the giant industrial complex which makes a free man punch his time card and ties him to a steel machine which promises to feed him if he will become an unprotesting slave. Freedom has been defined within the small circle of a religious or political tradition, within the framework of an economic or educational philosophy, so narrow and tight that only a revolution is able to bring about change. The stubborn or helpless are cut off, or excommunicated. The poor and ignorant are starved or ignored. The weak individual is used and manipulated by the strong. The nonconformists are said to be in heresy.

Heresy is another relic from the outmoded past. It is the intellectual touchstone upon which some religious or political or social faith is made to rise or fall. A heretic is one who rejects some truth that a government or a family or a church believes in. In the case of the Christian heretic, it does not matter how fruitful and godlike a man's life. The Christian criterion of judging a tree by its fruits is not enough. There must be assent to a body of doctrine. The man who gives blind and meaningless consent is said to have childlike faith. He does not wrestle with the meaning of a truth. He is not overwhelmed with the idea of God or the significance of Christ's divinity. He never thinks about it; he merely accepts it. It causes him no concern, so the religious body admits him as a son.

It is no different with the political body. The patriot is the man who will fight in Vietnam, who will pay his taxes, and who will build with them an altar of holocaust to murder helpless and unsuspecting men. To burn a draft card is heresy. To refuse to fight is a kind of treason. It is not in keeping with the nation of Lee and Grant and Teddy Roosevelt. It does not matter if a man has moved beyond political theories that were founded on fear and exploitation and arrogance. He is expected to conform to the dictates of his president, his employer, his college president, his family traditions, his religious heritage.

The man who rejects the truth which eludes his reason, or who at least withholds his consent, the man who questions the political system which says he is only permitted to be grateful for his right to vote, the man who despises the isolationism and nationalism that are called "patriotism" is heretical no matter what he does.

"Heresy" and "excommunication" are coward's words. They have lost their impact and meaning. To be a heretic can well mean that one is alive and responsible. To be excommunicated can well mean that one has made a mature and personal decision. How can a man who behaves as a Christian be heretical? How can a man who fights for the

Negro and refuses to fight a war be heretical? How can a godlike man who loves his neighbor be cut off from the synagogue or church? How can a man who treasures his right to honorable dissent be less a patriot? A life without love is the only heresy, a refusal to love the only excommunication. I look for heretics among misguided racists and pitiable philanderers, not among creative minds that struggle with the problems of God and meaning and try to love their neighbors as themselves. I look for the excommunicated among the greedy and the bigots and the self-righteous, not among the priests who took a wife or the gentiles who married a Jew.

There is no such absolute authority as that which excommunicates men and calls them heretics. It died somewhere in man's endless struggle to be himself. It only appears in such monstrous forms as concentration camps and Communist purges, Chinese communes and uncivilized prisons, or in jungle life among the beasts. To resist such authority, to wipe it out, is no mere challenge; it is a sacred duty in the name of man.

I am not an anarchist, nor is the spirited age in which I live anarchistic. I do not reject the notion of authority or its honest exercise. I only reject the leader who treats me like an ox or a piece of concrete. Maybe such a leader feels that man is not ready for the new freedom he demands. Maybe he believes that man is asking too much. Maybe he thinks that religion and morality and patriotism will disappear in the face of the contemporary onslaught. It does not really matter what he thinks or what I think. Man is going to find out for himself. Finally, after centuries, man sees the light and has a chance to look at himself without being cowed by religious authority or by the paternalism of an overprotective society.

Now man will take things in his own hands. He will make mistakes and pay the penalty within the framework of his own conscience, not in the courts where "heresy" and "excommunication" are frequent words. He will find authority enough in his responsibility to others, reproof enough in his failures and in the honest confrontation of friends. He will not pray away his loneliness in idle waiting. He will do something about it instead and at least attempt to find God in the love and meaning that is his right.

This new man is abandoning myths which have survived for centuries. He is not even asking for a professional evaluation of his revolutions. He will not be talked out of his demythologizing by learned theorists or angry commentators who hold him responsible for the increase in crime or the assassination of prominent and beloved men. He has learned to believe in himself, in his own *experience*, in his own new awareness that every man is his brother, in his own conviction, born of the electronic age, that the inequality of the past can and must cease.

He is aware of the crime in the streets. But he knows of the crimes of the religious myths that have excommunicated men and bound them in terror of an eternal "hell." He knows of the crimes of the political myths that have starved the poor and murdered millions of Jews. He knows the crimes of social myths that have deprived men of dignity and the right to work and read. He remembers well the tragic assassinations that made the world sad. But he also remembers the soldiers, Vietcong as well as Americans, who are dying for a myth in Vietnam, the Negroes who are dying because of the myth of white supremacy, the millions whose spirit has died with the crushing force of the religious myth.

This new man has appeared suddenly, but his roots lie

deep. The philosophers have been forming him for centuries and revolutions have been freeing him for years. His discoveries have given him confidence in his own powers and have taught him the value of his own experience. It is impossible to trace the ideas and events that spawned this new man, although everyone seems to be trying. I am not sure it is important to trace his roots, only to recognize that he is here. We can give credit to the French and American revolutions, the industrial transformation, the discovery and use of nuclear power. We can speak of the disillusionment produced by wars and the resulting philosophies of phenomenology and existentialism that brought philosophy from the world of concepts back into the world of men. We can give credit to the affluence produced by industrial growth and to the new leisure time that freed man from the fight to survive. We can praise the scientists, the historical and social critics, and the rebels—Luther, Darwin, Kant, Marx, Nietzsche, Freud, and their modern counterparts—who helped man to recognize his own dignity, his own capacity, who helped him to know that he is more important than any myth. Whatever produced him, a new man is here.

Man has never before had the freedom that modern life permits. And the results of this freedom, even at this early stage of development, impress me deeply. I love the openness of the young people I see, their ability to communicate directly, their honesty and emotional involvement in their world, their willingness to listen or to engage in dialogue. They have taught me a great deal. They do not live with the fear and bigotry that marked my life. I do not see them as less moral than the young man I was, or less moral than the young men I worked with at the beginning of my priesthood. Nor are they less dedicated, less idealistic, less responsible, or less concerned. They are better able to be friends, better able to determine what they want to do in life, better able to approach their parents and pastors and teachers. I am well aware of the irresponsible among the youth who would rather protest than work, who would rather talk than act. They are the drifters and cowardly rebels that the openness of new freedom brings. They are too immature to recognize the chance that they have, too proud to seek help, too lazy and indifferent to make decisions or to have goals. They are the leeches who live off the society they condemn or who receive support from the weak parents whom they criticize. But they do not represent the new spirit among the young. They are merely the excuse that permits the fearful conservatives to believe that nothing in life has really changed.

There is only one kind of authority that this new spirit among the young will accept. This authority does not demand as much and receives more. It trusts man. It confronts him and deals with him in the flesh, without relying on the outmoded conclusions of the past. It does not frighten or threaten man, nor make him guilty. It loves him.

Modern man will not only accept such authority, he will respect it as well. He will respect the father who wants to know him, who does not smother him with alien goals that seek the honor and praise of the family rather than his own honest aspirations. He will not love his father or mother simply because they have given him life and physical sustenance. He demands of them kindness and understanding, honesty and respect. He does not belong to them, he is not some showpiece with which they can win society's applause. He will not parrot their attitudes or memorize their every principle. He will not be what they want him to be, but what he has to be. He will be himself. He will not think their work and responsibility harder than his own. They will not make him guilty by telling him how much he owes them, nor will they frighten him with punishment or economic threats. He is not afraid to work, to struggle, to go it on his own.

He does not resent their discipline or honest punishment. He resents their arrogance and their refusal to be human. He does not admire them for hiding their weaknesses or for refusing to apologize or admit mistakes. Nor will he in youthful maturity accept the rules which have no meaning, the laws which have only authority's signature to give them worth. He will not accept his parents as perfect, as infallible, as beyond question or recourse. He will not accept material comfort in place of friendship and personal concern. He will not be deprived of privacy or the right to choose his own goals. He will not be forced to pay homage to the social emptiness that masquerades as recreation and pleasure. Nor will he barter away his personal freedom for a traitorous family peace. He will make his own mistakes and pay for them. He will form his own principles and pursue them. He will live his own life no matter what it costs in terms of a family relationship. He is himself before he is anyone's child, and he will not give his love where he cannot find respect.

Nor will I. No churchman will tell me to bow before some ordinance that does not make sense to me, or to embrace some doctrine without evidence. No president can demand my allegiance to a policy that offends my conscience. No father can order me to accept some principle which is contrary to my own faith. I am responsible to the dictates of my own mind and heart, and even if the cost shall pain me or kill me, I cannot do otherwise.

I will not define patriotism in the chauvinistic syllables of the past. Nor will I tolerate injustice dealt in the name of freedom. I know that my country is not all good, that its enemies are not all bad. I know that election to an office does not guarantee a man's intelligence or honesty, that it does not of necessity make him adequate for his job. I cannot accept an economy geared to war, a national budget that makes little of poverty and much of destruction and death. Nor will I accept the empty explanations for such horror or for some national commitment made in my name without obvious reasons—or supported by reasons inherited from a time when the nation considered itself invincible and omnipotent. I know that no such nation exists, and no scowling president will tell me otherwise.

Nor do I believe any society can be "great" if children are hungry, or if its sons and daughters are at war. It cannot be great if a black man is less than a white man, or if a growing abundance of material comforts does not bring a consequent growth of love and peace. A society is no greater than its compassion, its pursuit of justice, its guarantee of freedom and dignity for man. It is no greater than its humility, no greater than the poetry and art in the lives of its citizens.

No authority can command my love; no authority can demand my respect. I am man, and I am free. Any authority must listen to a man, know him, understand him, and merit his love. And in such an exchange there is beauty.

Once I could listen to the Church and its Pope and scrupulously fulfill every command. Once I could deny my inner feelings, my personal hopes, my weariness, my dishonesty, my disillusionment, my pain. I could hold another responsible for the injustice and horror perpetrated in the name of truth. I could hide behind the impersonality of a society without face or hands or heart. And I could call such docility "virtue," yet now I know it was only cowardice and an irresponsible attitude toward authority. Now I know that authority is only man, that it will listen when I demand that it listen, that it will respect me when I begin to respect myself. Now I know that when authority is absolute and infallible, it is only reflective of man's pessimism and fear. Such authority will no longer move me. Nor will it move the man of the global village.

Modern man is fighting against absolute authority of every kind. His cry is a battle cry. It is the cry of the man of the global village, the new man, the man who knows that every other man is his brother, the man who is determined to put an end to the narrowness and mythology that have forced men apart. This cry, this battle has only begun to be heard.

# 3. THE
# DEATH OF GOD

Man, in the course of his life upon the earth, has created thousands of gods. These gods have reflected his fear and helplessness in a vast and mysterious world. In the more primitive cultures, man had many gods because his fears were manifold. The forest and the sea frightened him, as did volcanoes and thunderstorms, so did hunger and war and death. Since man had limited knowledge, since he was unable to conquer his fears by himself, he looked for support outside of himself. He created gods who, if appeased, would make him happy, give him children and preserve their health, provide him with corn and meat, and rescue him from the dangers that lurked everywhere. Man appeased his gods with fine gifts, and he arranged the gods into elaborate mythologies and paid them homage. He stood before his petulant gods as a helpless child. The Greeks, for example, paid homage to Atlas whose shoulders supported the earth; they honored Poseidon who controlled the sea, and they relied on Ares to help him in war. In the East, men honored Indra, the warrior-god who generated lightning from the clouds and was master of the cosmic waters, and Enki the Sumerian god of flocks and fields.

Man could say that he had learned of his gods from secret

"revelations" or "sacred" traditions, but in reality the gods were created by the men who worshipped them. Each god was a reflection of the culture which produced him. Thus the Jewish god of the Exodus ruled like a bearded patriarch, not unlike Moses, and was the voice of wisdom and authority needed by a tribal people. Later on, at a time of a new and self-conscious monarchy, the same god appeared more as a king or sovereign. Similarly, in Egypt, the god Atum was fierce and powerful, as was the Pharaoh. In Rome the people transformed their emperor into a god.

Hence, to study the religious mythology of any culture is to discover the attitudes of its people, to know their hopes, their fears and frustrations, their self-image, their basic values, their environment. Even today, in the religions of primitive peoples, we find this to be true. Australian aborigines worship a black swan and a kangaroo. The Dakota Indians worship the *wakan* beings, the spirits that breathe in buffaloes and trees. In Labrador the Naskapi tribe honors the Master of the Caribou.

But in the variety of religious mythologies, beyond the gross superstitions and complex rituals, there is invariably an underlying awareness of the true God of mystery. This God is described as a power, a force, a kind of meaning that reaches beyond culture and defies accurate description. At times it is only a yearning, a subtle but intense hunger, a feeble cry of hope. But however apparent, it is more than a product of the culture; it is a kind of longing for the God of mystery Who is not made by man. In Polynesia, for example, despite a variety of cultural myths, the supreme god of the Maori, named Io, was not reduced to any human image, nor was man permitted to make offerings to him. In ancient Egypt the high god was the "maker of myself"; in ancient

India he was the ultimate resting place of the universe and could not be reproduced in art. And the Jews, unique in their religious genius, spoke of a spirit "hovering over the waters," its name too holy to be spoken, a being too complex and mysterious to be reduced "to a graven image." They were speaking feebly of the God Who is beyond all myth.

And modern man still speaks only feebly of Him. He can easily see through the cultural gods of the past and dismiss them. The gods of the Babylonians are dead; their god Marduk who built the heavens from the corpse of the dead god Tiamat is no more. Neither is the god of the Jews who "planted a garden in Eden" and created Eve from Adam's rib. Modern man finds little if any substance in the gods of some ancient culture: the god who is little more than a bearded Jew, or a kind of modern Pluto who rules the underworld, or a Byzantine king who glides solemnly through court rituals, or the god who is a sour Puritan critic. But he finds it hard to reduce into comprehensible words the universal longing of man for meaning.

Thus Paul Tillich speaks of "man's concern for the ultimate," and Camus describes the "fundamental human problem" of deciding "whether life is worth living or not." Martin Buber looks for this God in the uniqueness of a human friendship which does not use or manipulate its beloved. Even Vatican II, in a moment of exceptional honesty, asks, "What is man? . . . What is the ultimate significance of human activity throughout the world?"

This is man, now as always, searching for the God beyond culture and human traditions. This is man struggling to cope with the inevitable need that can make of life more than a meaningless continuum in the course of time. This is man struggling to find the God beyond statues and rituals and initiation rites. This God continues to live. He is the God Whom the Hindus call the "ancient Spirit," the high God of the Rhodesians, named Leza, Who is "merciful and does not get angry," the God of the Jews Who is "my shepherd," the Christian God who forgives "seventy times seven times." This God will never die. He survives all cultures, both primitive and sophisticated, because He has no nationality and is beyond all history. He can live in the global village.

It is the man-made gods that, if not dead yet, are destined to die. Granted, they seem to flourish for a time after the culture that produces them has passed away. Man clings to them lest he lose all contact with the true God of mystery and meaning Who lurks under the mythological forms. They are old friends whose moods he understands, comfortable idols that he can placate and control. Thus the Jews returned to the fertility rites of the neighboring Canaanites long after Moses insisted that Yahweh was the only God. The Romans offered incense to the "divine" emperor long after he was recognized as a mere human being. The primitive Indians in Mexico continue to offer food to the god of death even though they know that the shaman consumes it. And the Christians in Europe and America still whisper magic invocations and plead for salvation.

But such man-made gods are bound to die, as they always have. And prophets inevitably rise up to speed their death. Prophets are idol-smashers, assassins of man-made gods. The prophet Jeremiah forbade the Jews to "pour libations to alien gods." Mohammed struggled to convince a stubborn Arab world that "Whoever disbelieves in idols and believes in God has laid hold of the most firm handle." Christ, too, came as a prophet and said to the money changers in the temple, "Take all of this out of here and stop turning my Father's house into a market."

Initially, people have resisted prophets and have even killed them. But in time, the prophets made their mark because they appealed to the deepest part of man, where he yearns for the God Who is not "made by hands," the living God of mystery and meaning. In acknowledging this appeal, man turned, partially at least, from his idols and moved closer to the true God. He passed from the sacrifice of animals to the love of men. He smashed his golden calves, his totems, his charms. He drove out the sacred prostitutes and took away the witch doctor's powers. Then he was free again to feed the hungry, to comfort the lonely, to search again for the true God in pain and love.

While this rejection of idols has most often been a gradual process, it is possible to look back at the past and detect periods when it was cataclysmic and widespread. Moses lived in such a time, so did Jesus and Mohammed. So do we.

Man can no longer hide in remote areas and pay homage to his witch doctors and priests. Life will not permit men to live as strangers and to honor tribal deities as the living and true God. In the past, man had time to shed his idols. He could evolve gradually into religious maturity with a minimum of pain. But today, the death of the man-made gods, long predicted and talked about—is taking place with unprecedented speed. This is not just another bit of idol-smashing in history's record, but the most complete and radical that man has ever known. Nietzsche wrote about it in the last century, theologians and journalists have described it in recent years. But it is not, as they have termed it, the "Death of God." It is the "death of the gods" who usurped His place.

The man of the global village is aware of his own power. He is ready to face the fear of the unknown and refuses to build gods that only reduce his terror to empty symbols. He knows that he can bring an end to war, whereas the cultural gods have only requested prayers for peace. He knows that he can create social justice, whereas the man-made gods have only asked men to be patient with their poverty and starvation. The global village has no sects and does not need petty gods to sustain it. It has no magic beyond the marvels of man's creation, so it does not need ritual or sacrament. Man now rises up to tell the priests that their sectarianism and mythology produce the very climate of fear and narrowness in which suspicion and hatred grow. He is ready to dismiss the traditions that made static and absolute a given period in man's religious history. He is not even waiting for the prophets; he is scattering the idols on his own.

The man of the global village would be embarrassed if I were to suggest that he is doing a "religious" thing. He well may disavow all "religion," so angry and weary is he of its platitudes and superstitions. He is content to be doing the human thing, and that is to do the most "religious" thing of all. Whether he is a college student or a bank president, a housewife or a silent critic, he is the prophet of the death of the gods.

He does not fear to trust himself. He does not look to an authority to grant him permission to be free. He is not afraid of the consequences of human behavior, and he will not accept the universal principles adopted by frightened men who claim to be unassailable or infallible. Thus, for example, the authority of the Pope is dying after centuries of development. The Pope is obsolete. He is the reflection of a past culture which could not believe in itself. Such men needed a pope. Now his decisions are of less and less consequence. It is not merely a question of whether he speaks infallibly or not—this in itself is preposterous—but that he proposes to speak as a religious authority for millions.

Man now is not afraid to take an honest look at history. He knows that the Papacy was established by men, that it grew under the protection of secular powers. Peter was declared the first "Pope," and Scriptural authority was invoked to support his title. It was said that his journey to Rome, actually the result of turmoil in Antioch and Jerusalem, was precipitated by some "divine" call. This same "theology" cited a few historical texts from men like Ignatius of Antioch to support the Pope's place as spiritual sovereign. It related an example of a first-century "Pope" named Clement who chided the people of Corinth in a famous letter and thus "proved" his universal authority. By the fourth century, it was asserted that the Pope was the supreme and infallible authority established by God. Ambrose of Milan could write, "Where Peter is, there is the church."

The problem is that God did not put Peter there, Caesar did. What the culture had produced, theological arguments made "divine." Constantine, for example, supported the decisions of the Council of Nicea in 325 with his soldiery. The Pope served the emperor's purposes as a kind of spiritual Caesar, the symbol of religious unity in the Empire. Christianity was the state religion.

As a type of spiritual emperor, the Pope had powers that no man should have. He could, supposedly, unlock the gates of heaven. He decided which books belonged in the Bible. He wore jewels and was carried on a throne. He said Mass in elaborate ceremony and was fawned upon by religious courtiers who vested him and kissed his ring. The conversions he

commanded were not free commitments, but very often an
enforced loyalty to the Empire. The conquest of a barbarian
king often meant the religious "conversion" of his people.
The Pope was infallible; there was no power on earth that
could countermand his authority as long as he was on good
terms with the emperor.

And a strong emperor, like Charlemagne, even made
spiritual decisions. He determined the method of baptizing,
ordered attendance at Mass, even supervised the liturgical
ceremonies. When Leo III was elected Pope, Charlemagne
wrote to him as if to an underling and insisted that he "con-
duct himself properly, govern piously, and observe the can-
ons of the Church." Despite his multiple marriages and
mistresses, Charlemagne appointed the bishops, supervised
the Pope, and even decided intricate doctrinal questions like
the relationship of God the Father to God the Holy Spirit.
Charlemagne could not afford a weak Pope or an ineffective
spiritual leader, so he supervised his "infallibility" and as-
sumed the powers of his office.

Through the centuries, the Church recognized that it had
made an unholy bargain, for the pomp of the papal office
and its privileged position obscured the God of Love and
mystery. The monks of Cluny in France rose up to fight the
involvement of the Church in the feudal system. A unique
Pope in the twelfth century, Innocent III, called the worthy
bishops of his empire "dumb dogs who can no longer bark."
He demanded learning in clerics, and forbade them to live
with mistresses or to amass property. But he was fighting a
losing battle. The very structure of the Church, the very
office of the Pope and bishops, fashioned as they were in the
culture of the Roman Empire, were an unmanageable vehi-
cle of the Christian ideal, despite the well-meant efforts of an

occasional Pope like Innocent III. There would be too many popes who were not Innocent's.

The office of the papacy is the symbol of the kind of culture in which Christianity was spawned. The arrogance which modern man criticizes in the office of the Pope was once not arrogance at all. It was typical of the temper of the times. Man did not believe in himself; he was afraid to be responsible for his own moral behavior and his own salvation. So he looked to the Pope and worshipped the god of papal authority.

It is obvious that the Church would have had a different form if it had been founded in a democratic society. There would have been a representative form of government, not an infallible Pope who learned his leadership from an untouchable emperor. There would have been general religious principles and reasonable directions, not minute doctrinal codes and inexorable laws. Or, even if the Church had developed in a monarchical era, it would have been a different church if it had not attached itself to the Roman Empire. But the Church was the Empire's spiritual police force; it was the devoted teaching staff which dragged the barbarians into the world of culture, and it was the emperor's ally. It deserved an infallible Pope whose decisions were beyond all question.

This is not to deny the contributions the Church made to Western culture. It is not to ignore its libraries, its struggle to teach the illiterate to read and write. Nor is it to overlook the fact that much of the freedom and science we have today was spawned, at times unwittingly, through ecclesiastical leadership. Certainly it is not to overlook man's service of the God beyond culture, the God Who cared for the poor and homeless, the slaves and degraded, the God Who lurked under the mythology of an infallible Pope and brought men meaning and happiness. It was this God beneath the myth Who helped to prevent millions of men from rejecting papal authority centuries ago. The Church did give meaning to men's lives, it did build universities and feed the poor, it did support monasteries which were social and economic centers for the surrounding families.

But the Church had a fierce hold on frightened men as well. The Pope claimed to have the keys to the world beyond this one. Men could not look at the papacy as a cultural formation, so papal authority continued to live long after the culture which produced it had died. It survived the incredible Crusades, the Reformation, the French Revolution, man's very struggle for liberalism and democracy.

In Rome, at the Vatican Council in 1870, the Pope and his bishops and theologians declared the Pope infallible, insisting as a fixed dogma that he had absolute power over the entire Catholic Church. The Church did not want monarchy to end, it did not trust man to govern himself, it believed that freedom would lead only to immorality and anarchy. Thus it transformed the cultural derivative, papal infallibility, into a doctrine "revealed" by God. Some few bishops protested this "definition"; some few scholars left the Church. But the Council was over: "Rome has spoken and the case is closed."

Some years later in France, the Pope and his court supported a political movement called *L'Action Française*, which sought to restore the French monarchy. As in the Vatican Council, the Church refused to abandon the archaic culture that shaped its rigid constitution. It clung to its traditions in the name of "religion." The leader of *L'Action Française*, an avowed atheist named Charles Maurras, be-

came the Church's "intellectual leader for twenty-five years."
Maurras had no use for the Christian religion but he saw in
the cultural institution produced by the Empire an essential
ally. Maurras promised the Church the kind of world it had
known for centuries, and the Church offered him the rigid
framework in which his political absolutism would be most
effective. To Maurras the monarchy was the only effective
form of government; to the Church the monarchy was the
only cultural mold that could recreate the world in which its
infallible Pope was fashioned. So the Church held on to the
past, refusing to believe in man, and attempted to make
monarchical government the form of rule demanded by God.

Similarly, in early twentieth-century America, Rome accused the bishops of a new kind of heresy, called "Ameri-
canism." The American hierarchy was refused the right to
adapt to the genius of its own land. It was not to grow with
democracy; it was to cling to the world of Constantine and
Charlemagne, the world which dressed and formed them.
About the same time in Europe, Rome condemned the
Modernists, men who saw before their time that religion had
become autocratic and sterile, men who wanted religious
authority to reflect what man had discovered about himself,
men who submitted the religious myths of centuries to the
more critical tools of modern learning. Every Roman Catholic priest in the twentieth century was expected to take the
oath against Modernism, to promise not to be a man of his
own times. Today the "Modernists" are widely read and
admired, but the oath is still on the books. Their views are
heard everywhere; their condemnation is embarrassing to
scholars. But the infallible Pope who condemned them still
survives.

But today, the god of papal authority is finally dying. The

death rattles are now being heard. Some of them are embarrassing. One such was Pope Paul's excitment when the bones under the high altar of St. Peter's in Rome were said to be the true bones of the Apostle after whom the church was named. To Pope Paul this meant that Peter was really in Rome, that he had come there as the first Pope, that every bishop who succeeded him would be another Pope. It meant to Pope Paul that he, the successor of Peter, had the same "divine" commission and the same infallible power. Perhaps tomorrow he or his successor will find Caesar's bones mingled with those of Peter. Then perhaps he would have courage enough to reinter them together—forever.

The man of the global village does not know of any infallible men. One President made a mistake in Cuba's Bay of Pigs, another President has made a series of mistakes in Vietnam. Nor is he interested in the twentieth-century churchman who wants to unearth Galileo and to free him from condemnation by the Church. He knows that Galileo was right. That is enough. He also knows that the Church has been wrong as often as any other human institution. The god of infallibility cannot survive in the global village, neither can the awesome god who attempts to intimidate man with past cultural forms. No such form has been more effective than the myth of purgatory and hell. It has frightened men for centuries, ever since the superstitious age which made it the focal point of Christian faith.

The myth of hell and purgatory, and, indeed, limbo, is a vital part of my Judeo-Christian inheritance. He created the framework in which the Christian myth of the afterlife evolved. The ancient Jews spoke of a place called *sheol*; its exact meaning is hard to define. In former times it was said to be a "bottomless pit" in "the depths of the earth," a monster with jaws that could not be satisfied. The idea of *sheol* did not originate with the Jews, it was rather a part of their Semitic world. The man who enters *sheol* "will not ascend again," "shall not awake," "shall not see the light forever." Every man, indeed, went to *sheol*. It was not, as in later times, a place of punishment, but rather a place of inactivity and immobility for everyone who left the "land of the living." Neither was it a place of happiness. Even the Jewish patriarchs did not want to go there; they wanted to continue to live because a long life was the only available reward.

Later in Jewish history, some two centuries before Christ, there was a new note added to the concept of the afterlife. It appeared in the Book of Wisdom as well as in the Book of the Maccabees. There was mention of reward and punishment in the world beyond since the Hebrew notion of *sheol* now merged with the Greek idea of Hades. By the time of Christ there were many theories about the afterlife. A new word had also developed, *gehenna*, which most likely referred to a garbage dump outside of Jerusalem where rubbish was burned. This was the word that was frequently used in the New Testament for hell. If Christ spoke of hell personally, and not merely in the dramatic reflections of the Evangelists who wrote about him a generation or two after his death, he may well have used the word *gehenna*. Whatever the word used, the whole concept of eternal punishment was vague and mythological, the product of the merging cultures of Jerusalem and Greece and Rome.

It was in medieval times that the god of hell and purgatory became the very center of religious life. The medieval man was an apt subject for the most elaborate theories of the afterlife. An eclipse in 1315 made him fear the end of the world. The conjunction of Jupiter and Saturn precipitated predictions of all kinds. The plague of the Black Death in 1347 cut the population of Europe in half and sent man whimpering to pay homage to his magical god. Man was helpless before portents and omens of any kind; the fear of death became an obsession. Men spent hours meditating on the sufferings of Christ; sorcerers and witches became popular, and devotions to special saints who could rescue man from hell developed beyond control. Relics of the saints were prize possessions; the gaining of indulgences was perhaps the most popular devotion. Bands of penitents wandered through towns, lashing themselves till they bled—to atone for their sins.

In such a world the god of purgatory and hell could flourish, and the vagueness of Scripture and early Christian tradition about the next world could be built into elaborate systems. Dante could write of *Purgatorio* and *Inferno*; morality plays could delight the people when a god came down to rescue a soul from eternal torment. And without one word in the Scriptures, the doctrine of limbo could develop. Similarly, without any evidence that Christ said one word about purgatory, with scanty proof for any awareness of it in early Christianity, it could appear with full force. It modified the fierce concept of hell which had then developed. It gave man some chance to be "saved" despite the misery of his own humanity. The myth of hell and purgatory has lived until today. Men still preach about it; Masses are still said to free tormented souls, the Pope is still granting indulgences to quiet "divine" wrath. Men still tremble at the final judgment at which Christ, supposedly, will appear to pass sentence.

But this god—like the god of papal authority—is dying, and his death is long overdue. Now, man is concerned with the horror of this world and will take his chances on the next. He knows the hell of war, the purgatory of an unhappy marriage, the anguish of life. He cannot be concerned with the myths of another culture, with the god of fiery volcanoes and eternal hell. Such a god is too arbitrary to bother with, too obviously a myth to be worthy of theological discussion. He is dying and the man of the global village will put him in his grave.

Another prominent diety, the tax-exempt god, is dying too. Unlike the gods of hell and papal authority, he is defended by civil law and is doubly hard to dislodge. But like those other gods, he is the product of an ancient and alien culture. His roots lie in the privileged status that superstitious nations gave their priests. The Jews, for example, set aside an entire tribe, the tribe of Levi, to be used in the service of God. They were to take the place of every firstborn Jewish son who, according to their culture, belonged to the Lord. This particular tribe was then to be supported by the offerings of the people. This tribe did not have to work or fight; its entire obligation was to assist at the sacrifices and religious rituals.

The Christian cleric received the same exemptions for somewhat different reasons. The Jews exempted the Levites because the Jewish nation was a kind of theocracy and the worship of God was an accepted part of their culture. The Christian priest was exempted because Christianity was adopted as the state religion.

But even when Christianity is no longer the state religion, even when there is no state religion, religious exemption continues in our culture. It makes no sense to the man of the global village. If he does not care to practice some formal religion, he does not see why he should be obliged to pay homage through tax exemptions.

The Church in our society is a vested interest. Very often
in the process of assuming a moral position, it takes a political stance. Often the Church has its own schools which perpetuate its own myths and mold its own subjects. Such
schools and such churches should not be tax exempt. This is
to exempt household deities; this is to support the expensive
bureaucracies that modern religions have become.

There is a great difference between freedom of religion
and the privileged position of the tax-exempt religious institution. Perhaps it would be different if religions were engaged in universal works of charity rather than in the particular programs of proselytizing and "salvation." Why should
modern man be charged for the private cultural hangups of
religious groups? Why should religious ministers and priests
be exempted from military service? We are not ancient Jews,
nor are we medieval European Christians. We exempt religions from taxation, and yet we have nothing to say about
how religions use their funds. We permit them to exclude
worthy citizens from their programs of charity because they
do not profess the right kind of faith. Catholics can admit
Catholics into their schools in preference to non-Catholics.
We do not audit religious books; we know nothing of the
expenditure of funds. A religious group can erect a million-
dollar church and ignore the poor—all in the name of charity
and the tax-exempt god. A religious home for the aged can
compete with a home that is privately owned and not have
to explain why it charges as much or why it excludes people
who cannot pay the entire monthly bill. A parish can operate
an inferior school, hire teachers who are not qualified, and
demand that its subjects attend; and society must reimburse
the tax-exempt church for this religious act.

Increasingly, man sees the tax-exempt god as a cultural

relic. Man is anxious to see how long this god will survive if the coffers of Caesar are not opened to him. He does not see poverty among the churchmen, he does not see hunger or need in the ranks of the clergy, nor does he see them rushing in vast numbers to assist the poor or to bring an end to war. He sees them making bank deposits to preserve their superstitions and irrelevant myths. He insists that if they have an adequate product, men will pay for it, but only as they require it and use it.

The god of the blue laws, too, is a cultural overlay protected by society's codes. He is a relic of pharisaic religion and puritanical ethics. He is preoccupied with alcohol and gambling, divorce and dancing, and Sunday rest. In New York a man may have a few drinks in a bar until four in the morning, in Phoenix the glass is snatched from his hand at twelve-forty, in Richmond he is not permitted to purchase liquor in a glass at all. This makes no sense to the man who could have breakfast in New York, lunch in Richmond and dinner in Phoenix. In Washington, D.C., he must stop drinking on Saturday night at midnight, so he goes a few blocks away and drinks till two in Maryland.

The laws of gambling are equally as childish and are likewise a cultural hangover. Virginia forbids horse racing, so its ranchers are content to raise horses for the nearby tracks in Maryland and West Virginia. Reno and Las Vegas have become national shrines of gambling since so many states forbid gambling on cards or dice or roulette. Once such laws seemed to make sense to a solemn people who worshipped a puritanical and stuffy god. Now they are ridiculous. They have nothing to do with religion or moral behavior unless it is to tempt man to break the law. The Mafia and the similar crime syndicates that exist in every area of our country are supported by the blue laws. They supply men with the alcohol and gambling that these archaic laws forbid. Each Mexican border town has become an exciting "den of iniquity" for the same reason. These obsolete laws have helped to create the numbers rackets, the "afterhours" joints, the "private" crap games. They are an offense to any man of judgment, but they are solemnly enforced with the same childish zeal that produced them in another culture.

Divorce laws reflect the same senseless rigidity. They are the product of the same archaic culture. In America they provoke a bitter battle between husbands and wives who are asked to appear in court as adversaries. It is not enough that they simply want a divorce. The blue laws refuse to face the fact that divorces will exist, as will gambling and alcohol, regardless of laws.

Not only is man rejecting the gods of religious authority who oppress him and the puritanical gods who treat him as a child, but he also finds diminishing point to the ritualistic gods that reflect a dead culture. Once it seemed to make sense to dress ministers and high priests in special robes to symbolize their mystic power. The Book of Exodus describes the vestments that were to be made for Aaron and his sons, the "pectoral, ephod, robe, embroidered tunic, turban and girdle." Each detail of tailoring was prescribed by law. The religious ceremonies were described in lavish detail; the position of the altar and the offering of incense were not left to chance. And Christianity was equally ritualistic. Even today, bishops appear in public wearing slippers and long white gloves. In our culture, slippers are for the bedroom or for the beach, and long white gloves are evening wear for women.

The major religions still recite their archaic prayers; they still perform their outmoded liturgies with bows and gestures

to honor the obsolete god of ritual. Recently the Episcopalians revised their Communion service, and the Catholics offered alternate forms for the canon of the Mass. The
revisions are merely a simpler and more elegant version of
the same irrelevant invocations that came from another culture. Such ceremonies have no meaning now; they reflect
another world.

The flowing vestments embarrass me with their effeminacy
and remind me of a Shriners' convention or a fraternity
initiation. The stilted prayers and postures of the liturgy re-
call an oracle at Delphi. Candles suggest a birthday party or a
romantic table decoration. Altars speak of Druids and bleeding lambs. Blessings and sacramental rites conjure up Mac-
beth's witches and dying Jewish patriarchs surrounded by
their sons.

I can well understand that such rituals can evoke warm
memories of the past and can fill traditional hearts with
nostalgia. I can accept the fact that many people enjoy the
elaborate ceremonies much as they might enjoy a familiar
aria in an opera or a well-known scene in a favorite play. I am
even willing to admit that for many men the mystique of the
ritual has aesthetic value and echoes the mystery and holiness of God.

But I know, too, that locked within the very rituals themselves is a description of man's attitude and approach to
God. Rituals are eloquent expressions of how man must
come to God in servility and according to formulae. They
describe a man who appeased his god by passwords and
magic signs. They describe a god who is outside of man,
ruling like a Byzantine king in some exalted heavenly court.
They speak of a god who can "save" a man arbitrarily or
send him to an incredible "hell." They well may have

aesthetic appeal to some, but they reflect most clearly the
religious servitude learned in a culture when man was more
docile in his slavery.

Modern man refuses to grovel before such a god, to bow
and to kneel in a superstitious kind of subservience. He does
not look for his God in frozen prayers and in stuffy ceremonies. He does not seek protection from wandering devils
or ask blessings from "consecrated" hands. He does not light
candles or shake incense; he does not join in group incanta-
tions. He finds his God in the search for daily meaning, in
the struggle to learn to care, in the commitment to be responsible. He wants to talk to men, not to pray at them. He
wants to love men, not to hide from them in archaic rites.
He wants to know men, not to ignore them in his concern
for ritual. He is in search of the God Who makes men free,
and in his search he is preparing hundreds of cultural gods
for burial.

Oppressive gods, I am glad you are dead. You are the
feeble creation of hungry and frightened men. You starved
them even as you fed them; you built walls against their
neighbors even as you spoke of love. You are man at his
weakest and most dependent. You are man's intolerance, his
guilt and anxiety, his dishonesty and prejudice, his heartless-
ness, his resentment, his childish fear, his pettiness and
greed, his refusal to live in the present, his unwillingness to
be responsible for his own acts, his jealousy, his insecurity,
his inability to live with mystery and doubt. You are the
symbol of man's rejection of himself, his deepest lack of
confidence, his secret fear that he is not loveable in himself.
Now you are dying or dead. Now man has piled you on an
immense pyre to reduce you to the ashes of the earth from

whence you came. Soon he will stand over you and all the world will know of your death. And I will rejoice, and so will free men everywhere, for in the death of the cultural gods is the *birth of God.*

# 4. THE BIBLICAL MYTH

Every major religion has had its sacred books. Every major religion has had "sacred persons" in special contact with God. Gotama Buddha was such a person, and hence could say, "I am the holy one in this world; I am the highest teacher." Mohammed tells of a visit with the angel Gabriel, who appointed him Allah's apostle, and he speaks of special communications from Allah himself. Moses ascended to a high mountain and there "Moses spoke and God answered him with peals of thunder." Jesus, too, was in contact with God, and at the time of his baptism a voice from heaven was heard to say, "This is My beloved son in whom I am well pleased." In all of these cases, the special "revelations" from God were recorded in "sacred books."

Man could not question these books; he could not qualify them in the light of his own experience. He was asked to accept them as "absolutes" and to meditate upon them that he might find the truth. Once man was able to do this. For most of my life I did this. I could go to the Bible and reflect upon its teachings and stories and apply them to my daily life. I did not question the story of Adam and Eve, the murder of Abel by Cain, the transformation of Lot's wife into a pillar of salt. I believed that the origin of languages was traced to the tower of Babel, that Noah really built an ark, that an arm of the Red Sea literally parted to permit the passage of the Jews, that the walls of Jericho actually tumbled down with a resounding crash under the leadership of Joshua.

It was only gradually that I learned that many of the biblical stories were myths and that other peoples had a mythology similar to that of the Jews. I read the creation account believed by the ancient Sumerians (2000 B.C.), and although it is primitive and mythological, it contains enough similarities to the biblical account to put the Jewish myth in some perspective. The story of the flood among the Babylonians is obviously from the same remote source as the biblical story. And the Code of Hammurabi, dating from the seventeenth century before Christ, contains numerous similarities with the Jewish law and strongly suggests a common background.

For centuries man had not been able to put the Bible in any kind of context since little was known about the peoples of the ancient Near East. It was only after World War I that excavations were begun in earnest in this area. Some twenty thousand tablets were discovered on the site of ancient Mari, a city on the Euphrates, and revealed a flourishing life in the Mesopotamian world some three thousand years before Christ. There were important discoveries at Ur in ancient Chaldea, reputed to be the city from which Abraham came. Work was done in Egypt, in Syria, in the ancient biblical cities. Ancient languages were deciphered. People who were once a mystery were better understood. The religious world of Christ, long subject to pious guesses in many areas, became much clearer with the discovery of the Dead Sea Scrolls after World War II. But even now, the work is only beginning.

With these important archeological discoveries, the work of biblical criticism became an important science. The critics were hard on the religious myths that man had learned to accept as true. The Exodus, which is the key to the Jewish nation, could now be seen as a tribal migration. There is hardly a mention of the Jewish Exodus in Egyptian history. The dates and circumstances are only guesswork. But the Jews, sparked by their religious genius, had turned it into sacred history. Moses confronted Pharaoh, he inflicted plagues on the Egyptian people, he demanded release from slavery in the name of God. When the Jews wandered in the desert for two or three generations, God was their leader. When water was found, it was seen as a miracle worked by Moses. When the tribal laws were enacted to build a strong nation and to keep the Jews apart from the dissipation of other desert peoples, it was reported that God had addressed Moses on Mount Sinai. The whole nation entered a kind of covenant with its desert God, and circumcision, a common practice among the ancients, became a religious rite to signify this pact.

This is not to say that there is no factual basis for the Jewish religion. It is only to say that it does not now appear that it came from the "revelation" of God, but from the genius of a gifted people. All the events of history were interpreted in a religious sense, and this is what is meant when we speak of "sacred history." Nations who resisted the Jews were seen as the enemies of God when they were only men attempting to protect their homes. The cruelty of the Jews, in destroying cities and massacring the inhabitants, became a kind of religious sacrifice to God called *herem*. A hailstorm that helped the Jews in battle was a kind of bonus sent from God. The passage from tribal existence to monarchical government was interpreted as a refusal to trust God. Victories in war were given by God; defeats were inflicted for not following His leadership. Even monotheism, for which the Jews struggled so long and hard, was not interpreted as a unifying political force, but a simple response to a revelation.

This is not to deny the beauty of the Old Testament. This is not to overlook the power of its myths and the spiritual heights of its prophets. It was Isaiah who wrote in the name of God, "I am sick of holocausts of rams and the fat of calves . . . help the oppressed, be just to the orphan, plead for the widow." It was Jeremiah who wrote, "I am Yahweh, I rule with kindness, justice and integrity on the earth." It was David who sang, "Yahweh is my shepherd, I lack nothing." The Old Testament rings with the fervor of a religious people. But it also rings with mythology, archaic and superstitious ritual, narrowness and national pride, cruelty and legalism. It is a high point in the writings of sacred history. It is an immortal book. It is the record of the unparalleled religious evolution of the Jews. But it is not the "word of God."

Nor is the New Testament. It cannot be understood except through the eyes of Jewish history. The men who wrote it were Jews, steeped in the law and traditions of their Jewish past. There is hardly reason for believing that God spoke to them directly; there is every reason for believing that they merely reacted as religious writers to the life and teachings of Christ, to the religious needs of their own times, to the problems they faced within their own religious communities. Always they were individuals reacting as distinct personalities to Christ and Christianity. They did not write biographies; they wrote "sacred history," interpreting the events of Christ's life within the framework of their own Jewish experience. They did not hesitate to use sources in telling their stories. Luke makes mention of them at the beginning of his Gospel. Both Luke and Matthew borrowed heavily from Mark. Mark in turn made use of an Aramaic version of Matthew and of material derived from the sermons of Peter. All made use of collections of the "sayings of Jesus" which were circulated before the Gospels. Each wrote for a special audience at a special time.

Mark wrote primarily to a non-Jewish world and stressed heavily the miracles that Jesus worked. Mark was a disciple of Peter and likely learned from Peter that the wonders of Jesus impressed the Romans. Matthew, on the other hand, wrote to the Jews, and he stressed the fact that Jesus was the Messiah promised in the Old Testament. Many of the events in Christ's life were seen as the fulfillment of some Old Testament prophecy. John the Baptist was said to be the Elijah who, according to Jewish tradition, was to return to the earth. Christ would be in the earth three days like Jonah was three days in the belly of the whale. The mothers weeping for their children slain by King Herod fulfilled the prophecy, by a strain of the imagination, of Rachel weeping for her children. Christ was seen as the new Moses who went up on a mountain with his disciples and was "transfigured before them." He also ascended a hill to reveal to the crowds the new and more perfect laws which would replace the commandments of Moses. Christ was the "son" of King David, the supreme prophet of Israel.

Luke, the most accomplished and human of the evangelists, emphasized heavily the gentleness of Christ and incorporated many of the "sayings of Jesus." He also stressed Christ's role as Saviour and made Jerusalem, the holy city, the center of Christ's ministry. Jerusalem, with all of its traditional meaning in the life of the Jews, was the only fitting place for the new and supreme sacrifice, the death of the Redeemer, to take place.

The Gospel of John stands alone and was written some three generations after the death of Christ. John was much influenced by the contemporary literature which has only recently come to light in some of the Dead Sea Scrolls. Thus he made frequent reference to the place of "knowledge" and to the struggle between "darkness" and "light." The Gospel of John is more subtle than the others and was written to a flourishing Christian community, but one that was suffering from the Roman persecutions as well. There is less emphasis on the physical aspects of the miracles of Christ and more on their deeper meaning as "signs." Thus, for example, when he wrote about the multiplication of the loaves and fishes, his story became a complete discourse on the liturgical rite of the Eucharist. He discussed more thoroughly the meaning of baptism and contrasted it with the more feeble rites of the Old Testament. The actual story of the sufferings of Christ was abbreviated, but there is a long discourse on the hostility of the world to the Christian. And since John had witnessed the destruction of Jerusalem and its temple by the Romans, and had seen the decline of the Jewish religion, he had Christ cleansing the temple at the beginning of his public life rather than at the end as did Matthew.

Thus John and the other Evangelists were not biographers, not simple chroniclers or objective historians. They could "rearrange" historical details to fit their theme; they could emphasize aspects of Christ's life which suited their own reasons for writing. They could inject their own personalities. They were religious propagandists who wrote "sacred his-

tory" in order to establish the power and the authority of
Christ and to lend support to their own leadership in the
Christian community. If persecutions were a threat to the
Christians, they wrote about Christ's attitudes toward suffering. If there were Jewish converts who still insisted on circumcision before baptism, they wrote about the end of the
Jewish religion. There is no factual basis for believing that
they had any special "revelations." Similarly, there is no such
basis for believing that Christ himself was in any occult
contact with God. More and more, the discovery of literature
and religious customs contemporary with Christ helps us to
see him as a man—unique and a genius—of his own times.
The Roman historian Suetonius only mentions in passing a
certain "Chrestus," and sees him as but one of many Jewish
preachers and "wonder-workers." The real power of Christ
came after his death. During his life he was very much a man
of his time.

It is not unusual to read of miracles surrounding the life of
such a man. The Jews had been waiting anxiously for a Messiah, a deliverer, since the nationalistic days of Judas Mac-
cabeus two centuries before. There was a vast literature that
sprang up during this period dealing with the messianic
theme. The Jews had every kind of idea of what the Messiah
would be, but generally they saw him as a man of militaristic
strength and personal power. It was not unusual for disciples
to gather around a given claimant and to attribute to him
miraculous powers. Jesus was not a Messiah of the most
popular variety, since he was a "peaceful" Messiah who had
no intentions of overthrowing the power of Rome. He would
suffer for his people and teach them, but his kingdom was
"not of this world." Still, his personality attracted crowds
and devoted disciples. His fame grew throughout the land
and the stories about him grew as well.

But the real myth of Jesus grew with the New Testament. The story of his life in public was transformed into "sacred history." His birth was described in the mythological terms reserved for heroes and great prophets. He was more than Moses, who was found among the reeds by Pharaoh's daughter. He was born in a stable and seers from the East came to worship him. An angel warned his father that Herod was determined to slay him, although Herod could hardly be concerned about a Jewish baby born of peasant stock. He was forced to flee into Egypt—a kind of reverse of the original Exodus. Every known event in his life was symbolic, filled with special meaning.

When he visited the temple as a child, he astounded the doctors with his learning. When he was baptized, a voice from heaven spoke. When he began to preach, he was led into the desert by Satan and kept there forty days in hunger, like his people who remained there after the Exodus for forty years. He worked every kind of miracle to astound the people, healing the blind, curing the deaf, and raising the dead. Yet, despite his wonders and the force of his words, most men did not listen to him. He was deserted in his death; he wandered through the streets of Jerusalem carrying a cross and no one came to his assistance. On the third day after his death, he rose from the dead and was seen by more than five hundred people, although one of his closest friends, Mary, did not recognize him when she saw him in the garden.

Scholars now recognize that most of his miracles were merely hearsay or natural events to which the people gave some mystic explanation. But most refuse to believe that his Resurrection from the dead is in the same category. Dr. Hugh Schonfield, author of the *Passover Plot*, has gone so far as to suggest that the disciples of Jesus removed his body from the grave and made it appear as if he had risen. This, to me, compounds the problem. Why did Jesus have to rise from the dead at all? Why in the light of what we know of "sacred history" could not the Resurrection of Christ be merely a contrived symbol of his victory? What would a physical resurrection accomplish except to make him more than human and to replace the simple faith of his disciples with an astounding vision?

It is an interesting experience to attend a lecture given by one of the modern Scripture scholars who believes in the Resurrection as a physical miracle. He will discuss the miracle of the changing of water into wine as a popular tradition and as a symbol of the transformation of Judaism into Christianity. He will talk about the miracle of the loaves and fishes and dismiss the physical fact with an emphasis on the word of God which feeds the starving multitudes. He will call the healings of the blind and the deaf literary devices that attempt to show the effect of Christ's teaching on hardened men. And he will support his rejection of these miracles with parallels from other traditions and with a discussion of the kind of literature that the Bible is. All of this I endorse, and it makes the Bible, not a book of fables, but a classical work of religious significance.

But then, when he comes to the Resurrection, suddenly the Gospel narrative becomes a physical fact. He says that Christ returned to strengthen the faith of his disciples, to provide them with unity and new leadership, that the evidence is overwhelming. I do not find the evidence overwhelming, especially when it is the written report of "believers." Nor was it necessary for the faith of the disciples if they were impressed with Christ's teachings about forgiveness and love. The parables alone would guarantee him immortality; the beatitudes have been enough to inspire millions of lives. Sayings of Jesus have become household mottoes; his equanimity in the face of death and his courage in the face of life have been a model for centuries. Paul could say, "If Christ is not risen, our faith is in vain," but if he was referring to the physical resurrection of Christ, I do not believe him.

I do not require that kind of faith. Nor do I have to be knocked from my horse as Paul was and receive a special vision from Christ. I do not believe in Paul's vision, nor do I believe in Christ's physical resurrection. I believe that he somehow conquered death; I believe that he gave millions of men hope that they never had before. I believe that he has had an undying effect on Western civilization, and that he has made an indelible mark on my own life. But to believe that he rose from the dead is to reduce him to a myth of sacred history, it is to confuse the symbol for the fact, it is to misinterpret the superstitious times in which Christ lived.

For centuries the Bible was accepted as a book of historical truth. Its fables were understood as fact. It was only with a study of the literature of the time that man began to realize that "sacred history" had none of the rules that we demand today. Historical criticism of the Bible is not very old, and Catholic scholars were forbidden to apply their knowledge to the New Testament until after World War II. It took them a long time to catch up with the world of scholarship. Now they can begin to understand that the biblical writers were unscientific "children of their own day," and talented artists of "sacred history."

Even when the biblical critics began to reveal their conclusions, there was a tremendous resistance on the part of the people. They had learned the biblical stories in childhood; they had celebrated them on the major feast days of the year, and they had taught them to their children. The critics had to be cautious with their conclusions or they would be dismissed by the people. The Catholic critic had an additional problem. For generations Catholics had used the Bible as a kind of textbook to support traditional doctrines. They had sought out texts to establish the virginity of Mary and her assumption into heaven. They had looked for passages to make marriage a sacrament and to support their views on the last rites. They had searched for a text to lend credence to purgatory and limbo, another to prove that the Pope is infallible and that priests had the power to forgive sins. Catholics had reduced the Bible to a code of absolutes, and biblical criticism could bring the whole religious structure down on their heads.

It has not been my intention here to *disprove* the Resurrection or the physical miracles of Christ. No man can do that. This is not an area of proof or disproof. I have merely stated that I do not believe in the Resurrection as a physical fact, nor do I accept the countless miracles of Christ. I believe that they are the products of the age in which Christ lived and are characteristic of the type of literature that was written to reveal him to men. Nor do I believe that the Bible is *the* word of God. I can only accept it as the important religious experience of men who lived nineteen centuries ago and their reactions to the events surrounding the history of the Jews and the life of Christ.

It is unfortunate that the Bible has been seen as some kind of "supernatural" invasion of man's religious progress. Those that see the coming of Christ as a "divine" visitation outside the normal framework of history do man an injustice. History was ready for Jesus Christ. Given his own creative genius, there is an adequate explanation for his work and teaching in his own Jewish culture. Few of his ideas are so unique that there is not clear evidence of them in the literature of his Semitic tradition and in the religious fervor of his own age. This is not to say that he was not a man before his times. This is not to say that he did not possess unparalleled insights. It is only to say that the religious history and genius of the Jewish people could produce a Jesus Christ some two thousand years ago. It is my contention that this is exactly what happened. I do not believe that "God" should be given credit for what man can accomplish by himself. Nor do I believe that man would have accepted the teachings of Jesus Christ if he had not been conditioned by his own culture. Man listened because history and experience had made him ready to listen. Jesus was not a *divine* being superimposed on his own era. He was an extraordinary prophet of his own age.

The whole idea of a "supernatural" revelation from God to man is a primitive and an artificial one. Man does not need "revelation." He does not need God to speak to him in special visions or in mystic apparitions. God did not appear to Moses in a "burning bush" or speak to him in "thunder" upon the mountains. Neither did God speak to the Jewish prophets or to Mohammed in some unique "revelation." He did not reveal Himself to Paul in the "seventh heaven," nor did John receive some ethereal transfusion of divine wisdom while writing the Apocalypse (Revelation). All that Moses offered men, all that John or Jesus provided, can be well explained by man's own progress in self-knowledge. Man learns to know God as he learns to know himself. Assuredly he requires some voice to make his secret thoughts known; he needs some prophetic genius who can transform his own tenuous hopes and dreams into verbal form and concrete substance. He needs poets and evangelists, interpreters and philosophers, prophets and even seers if you will. But he does not need a "revelation" from God.

God speaks in man's own struggle to be himself. God speaks in man's stubborn effort to translate his love for his own wife and children, his love for his own city and state, into a love of the whole world. God speaks in the struggle of the Negro for justice, in the effort of modern man to protest all and any war, in the rage of modern society to be free from institutions that have lost their meaning, to be free from traditions that have lost their roots, to be free from laws that only make it harder to love.

I do not believe that Moses had a "revelation," or that the Virgin Mary appeared to some shepherd children of Portugal or to Bernadette of Lourdes. I do not believe that God sent messages to Paul of Tarsus or Jesus of Nazareth. God does not invade our world and interrupt its course. He speaks only gently in the efforts of all men to be mature, to grow in wisdom and love. The source of "revelation" is man's own heart and mind, and the appearance of a prophetic voice means simply that man is continuing to grow.

It is unfortunate, too, that the Bible has become some kind of absolute. It is unfortunate that men have made it the ultimate vision in the religious development of man. Even though history bears witness to the various "kinds" of Christianity that have existed in every century, man still stands before the Bible as before some vision of the all-holy God. To say that the Bible is only the record of an important stage in man's religious growth is not to discredit the record or the man. I can read the Bible, as I sometimes do, and be inspired by its pages. But I cannot go to it as though it were an unyielding oracle who relates once and for all the will of

God. This is to make of the Bible a myth, a pretentious idol, a barrier to creative and personal thought. When the Bible tells me that divorce is forbidden except in the case of adultery, it tells me more about first-century society than about Christ. But to insist that the biblical teaching on divorce is irrevocable is to deny all of the progress that modern man has made in his understanding of the relationship between husband and wife. It is to produce the very kind of quibbling that religious sects have engaged in for centuries.

When the Bible insists that widows should not remarry, it helps me to understand the attitude of Paul when he thought the world was soon to end. When the Bible tells me that women should cover their hair in the churches and keep silence, it amuses me with its archaic customs. When it discusses the importance of sacrificial offerings, it relates to a Semitic background which I do not share. When it speaks of the "gift of healing" or the "gift of tongues," when it describes the sufferings of "hell" or the manner of the Resurrection from the dead, when it discusses the Last Judgment or the cosmic phenomena at the end of the world, I only understand a little better the kind of world in which the Bible was written.

People will say that I do not have "faith." What they mean is that I do not have the docility to accept blindly the Bible apart from its environment. I truthfully do not want such "faith." It is not to Mark's credit that he could write of the miracles of Christ. He lived in an age when there was nothing extraordinary about a miracle. So did Peter and Paul and Luke. They could see signs everywhere; they knew nothing of science, nothing of modern psychology, nothing of medicine or chemistry. They lived in a world in which

wonders of all sorts were the panoply of a great man. They
believed that Moses was a great man and that he worked
miracles with his staff. They believed that he filled the land
of Egypt with frogs, that he turned the waters of the river
into blood, that he ordered the waves to engulf Pharaoh and
his chariots. And in Christ they saw a greater man than
Moses, a man who worked greater marvels. To such men, a
miracle was no problem. Nor even now is it a problem
among primitive peoples and superstitious children who
escape modern acculturation. But it is a problem to me and
to millions of modern men, and it has nothing at all to do
with faith.

I will not accept the biblical myth, but I will accept the
Bible. I will not accept the concept of "inspiration" that says
that God worked with the sacred writers in some special way
when they wrote down their account of Christ. I simply
accept the sacred writers as great religious authors who offer
me their first-century reflections on the life of Christ. I must
distinguish in their offerings the kernel from the shell. I must
determine what is a permanent truth and what is a cultural
bias. I must compare their experience with my own and
decide the direction of my own life.

And when I see Christ beyond the biblical myth, his words
and memory help me to realize that I count. I count because
I am a man, not because I am a Catholic or a Christian, not
because I was baptized or ordained a priest. I count more
than the lilies of the field, more than the birds of the air. It
does not matter if I am wise or wealthy, uneducated or poor.
It does not matter if my life is scarred with a thousand
failures, if I am sentenced to the gas chamber or abandoned
by my family. I am of value; I am worth the world. I am
worth the ransom of kings and more. I am worth the life of a
friend.

I can go to the Bible, not as a court of law, not as a code of ethics that some angry man shakes in my face, not as an unswerving absolute, not as a textbook that some Fundamentalist uses to hide his fear or unawareness of the modern world. I can go to it to get a picture of a man named Jesus Christ. I can accept the fact that he is dead, that I am alive, and recognize that the only memory I can have of him is in the words of his biographers. I do not look to him for every answer; I reflect on the words written about him and find meaning. I do not care if they are inspired or special words; I only know that they are important words that aid me in my search for God.

Jesus is not the only one who makes me feel this way, but somehow he seems to do it better than the rest. And in my loneliness, in the agony of my own search, I spend a few moments with his words. He warns me of pinning my hopes on money or material success in place of meaning and love. Yet, he does not ask that I turn my back on the good things of the world. He does not overpower me, or make me feel immoral or worthless. I watch him weep at the death of a friend and know that he is like me. I watch him comfort a widow, give a blind man hope, a cripple courage, a leper dignity and respect.

He tells me not to fear the judgment of any man. He tells me not to pay homage to hypocrisy, not to be paralyzed by fear. He has no special powers; the awe of his biographers has provided these. I could not accept him if the wind and sea obeyed him, if he rose from the dead or multiplied loaves. I can accept him as he is, sensitive and understanding, pragmatic and concerned, seeking out pain and loneliness and offering the healing of his own manliness. And his manliness is beyond all myth.

For the myth of Jesus, and the myth of the Bible, is as

nothing compared to the reality. It takes no "faith" to accept
a myth. It is not hard to believe that a man walked on water
or another man rose from the dead. I do not believe it, but it
would take no courage to believe. What does it matter if
water is changed into wine, or if a storm is stopped in the
midst of the sea? But it matters terribly if there is "neither
Jew nor gentile, neither slave nor free." It matters terribly if
"those who mourn shall be comforted," if "the gentle shall
inherit the earth," if "the eye is sound, the whole body shall
be full of light." Marvels do not matter, only love and hope
and honesty and courage. And these are what a man finds
when he looks beyond the biblical myth.

Some time ago I made an appearance in court. I watched a
man swear "on the Bible" that he would tell the truth. I was
sorry that he had to pay homage to an old-fashioned custom
and swear at all. But I was particularly sorry that he had to
swear "on the Bible." The Bible is a book, granted a special
and priceless one, but not a religious idol to be sworn upon.
It is not a book to be incensed in Catholic ceremony or to be
paraded in a courtroom. It is a book written for men, by
men, with all the passion and love and feebleness of men.
Man in his history has turned it into a myth. That is why he
could be lost in the pettiness of its detail and forget that its
only important message is one of love. That is why he could
use it as a "holy" club to beat his fellowmen into line. That
is why it could divide man from man and be carried by
opposing armies as they tried to murder each other in war.
Day by day the Bible is becoming a human document, a
proud record from man's religious past. Soon men will not
swear upon it, they will only feel responsible to improve
upon it, and will cease treating it as an oracle from God.

Our generation has a bible all its own, a bible that is being written every day in the struggle to bring justice to the help-less and to end war. It has its own psalmists in the folk singers, Dylan and Baez, whose songs "Blowin' in the Wind" or "Be Not Too Hard" have more meaning for modern man than the chants of a David: "Loudly I cry to God, loudly to the God who hears me." The draft-card burners and the protesting college students are more mean-ingful and equally as prophetic as the Ezekiel with his vision of dry bones, or the Jeremiah with his smashing of a clay jug to symbolize God's displeasure with His people, or the Hosea who married a whore to symbolize the Jews' un-faithfulness.

This is not to say that the Bible has lost its meaning; it is only to say that the Bible can be put in perspective and can be brought up to date. We can read about Job who lost his home and family and accepted his fate while lying miserably in a pit of ashes. We can contemplate his vision of the world, the new awareness of life's uncertainty that suffering brought, the utter misery that moved him to cry out, "May the day perish when I was born." But every day I can see Job in the suffering of the Negro. I can see Job's frustration and anguish in the ghettoes, in the crowded rooms, in the in-ferior schools, in the unemployment and poverty of the Negro. I can see the ulcerous sores of Job in the rat-bites on babies' arms and in the hopeless look in tall men's eyes. I can see Job's patronizing friends in the white supremacists who offer sophisticated theories and unenforced laws instead of help. I can also see a new and modern Job who is not satis-fied to wait for God to restore his life. I see a Job who is ready to rage and revolt to win justice.

I see Isaiah's call for justice in the throng of voices that refuse to tolerate the war in Vietnam. I see Jesus' beatitudes in the extended arms of a Pope John, in the quiet strength of a Martin Luther King. I see Paul's description of love in the dedication of the young to a life beyond the nationalism and self-interests of generations past. I see John's vision of "light" in modern man's new awareness that every person counts. I see the agony of the passion of Christ in the assassination of a president and in the broken heart of a nation. I see this same passion in a divided Germany, in an isolated Berlin, in the poverty of a village in Peru. I see it especially in the senseless devastation of a tiny country called Vietnam.

In seeing the bible of my own day, I can read the Bible of generations past. I can respect the leadership of Moses, the courage of Abraham, the beauty of Isaiah, the wonder of Jesus, the gentleness of John. But I can also see the modern struggle to liberate man and to give him the dignity that is his due. And in seeing this, I can go to the Bible, but not as a religious absolute, not as a static description of a final "revelation" from God. I can go to it not as a myth that forbids me to reflect on the experiences of my own life, but as the religious experience of an earlier and special age. I can see its wisdom and beauty, and I know that even now I am sharing in its growth and development.

# 5. THE
# SALVATION MYTH

One of the biblical myths that deserves special attention is that of salvation. It is a very central part of the biblical faith, and it pictures man as standing sinful and guilt-ridden before God. Man is born in sin and is prey to thousands of temptations and legalistic impurities that only serve to push him farther from his God. He is confronted with the inevitability of death. Only God Himself can save him.

The salvation myth evolved from man's awareness of evil in the world. Seeing no reason for sickness and death, for murder, theft, and hatred, philosophers in every culture attempted to explain them. Some, like the Persians, described two principles of creation, one a god of light, the other a god of darkness. Man contained within himself particles from each god; his existence was a constant warfare between these two opposing forces. The ancient Babylonians pictured the serpent as taking away the plant of immortality from their hero Gilgamesh, thus leaving man to flounder in his own evil and ignorance. The Jews shared the theme of the serpent in their story of creation and pictured Adam as being tempted by the cunning reptile.

But in the Judeo-Christian understanding of evil, man appears not only as tempted but as fallen. It was held that

evil resided in the heart of man. The Book of Job is a classical treatise on the problem of evil. Job asked, "Who can
bring the clean out of the unclean?" And the answer: "No
man alive." King David said, "My guilt is overwhelming me,
it is too heavy a burden; my wounds stink and are festering,
the result of my folly; bowed down, bent double, overcome, I
go mourning all the day." Jeremiah said, "Well you know,
Yahweh, the course of man is not in his control. . . . Cor-
rect us, Yahweh, gently, not in your anger or you will reduce
us to nothing." Even problems of hygiene and sickness were
somehow seen as evidence of man's impurity. A woman was
declared legally "unclean" after childbirth and was obliged to
come to the temple to be "purified." All kinds of physical
occurrences—such as burns, boils, chronic skin disease,
rashes, and loss of hair—were to be "examined" by the
priest. Certain animals were declared "unclean," for example, the pig, and to eat its flesh made a man legally "impure."

And in the Christian tradition, the Apostle Paul said,
". . . every single time I want to do good it is something evil
that comes to hand . . . my body follows a different law
that battles against the law which my reason dictates." In the
fourth century, Augustine wrote in his *Confessions* of his
own helplessness in the face of evil. Luther, in the sixteenth
century, described the "damned mass" of his own corrupt
flesh, and Calvin was suspicious of the evil contained in
human pleasure.

This is man in the Judeo-Christian tradition. Weak and
sinful, he cannot find peace within his own heart. He requires salvation through the help of his God.

From the earliest times, man's salvation came from sacrifice. Sacrifice was the putting to death of a victim to acknowledge God's dominion and mastery over all of life. The

death of the victim was man's way of admitting that he himself did not deserve to live.

Some peoples, such as the Semitic followers of the god Baal, offered human sacrifice. In the ninth century B.C., a man named Hiel rebuilt the city of Jericho. He killed his eldest son and put his body in the foundation of the reconstructed town, and he placed the body of his youngest son at the base of the city gates. This sacrifice supposedly assured evil men of God's protection. The Canaanite neighbors of the Jews were accustomed to sacrificing children. Numerous Indian tribes offered the fairest maiden in the community to appease the wrath of God.

Such human sacrifice was forbidden among the Jews. The familiar story of Abraham, who took his son Isaac to the top of a mountain and was ready to slay him before an angel stayed his hand, reflects the Jewish tradition forbidding human sacrifice. Among the Jews, as among many people, animals were sacrificed to God in place of man. The kind of animal was determined by the culture of the people. Thus the Ainu tribe originally from Siberia sacrificed a bear; in the Deltaic rituals of Asia, a horse was offered, and one ancient Roman sacrifice included "favorable owls, favorable crows," a male and female woodpecker. The Jews, in addition, offered fruit, grain, and incense. But usually the Jews killed lambs, goats, and bulls. The key to the sacrifice was the shedding of blood since the ancients believed that life was in the blood. Sinful man owed his life to God; vicariously he offered the blood of beasts.

The ritual of the sacrifices differed. There was a *holocaust* in which the flesh of the animal was completely burned, a *peace offering* in which part of the flesh of the animal was returned to the man who offered it to signify God's approval, and a *sacrifice of atonement* in which man placed his hands on the animal to transfer his guilt to the beast. But the shedding of the blood remained the heart of the sacrifice.

And by this sacrifice, man was "saved." To be "saved" meant many things. It meant that man was God's friend, that he was approved and worthy. Usually such salvation was temporary. Among the Jews it meant that he was free to be a member of the religious community and to pray with the rest of the "good" people. It meant that he would live long upon the earth, and, at a later time, it meant that he would know peace after death. To Christians it meant that he was living in the "grace" of God, that he was able to do a godlike work among men, that he would be spared the torment of an eternal hell and know the happiness of heaven.

Sacrifice as the key to salvation explains Christianity's view of the crucifixion of Jesus as a sacrificial death. This was only natural since Christianity originated in Judaism. The Christians drew a special parallel between the death of Jesus Christ and the death of the lamb which the Jews killed when they departed from the captivity of Egypt in their celebrated Exodus, or Passover.

On the night before their departure from Egypt, the Jews were instructed to select a lamb (or goat) from their flocks. The animal was to be a one-year-old male without blemish, and the blood of the beast was to be sprinkled on the doorposts of the Jewish homes so that the angel, who would kill the firstborn son of every Egyptian family, would spare the firstborn among the Jews. It was the *blood* of the lamb that saved the Jews, and the firstborn son was said to belong in a special way to the God Who saved him.

Christ became the new lamb of the "passover" from death to life in Christian symbolism. He became the "saviour," the perfect lamb whose blood would withhold the wrath of God. He was without blemish like the lamb, he was born without sin of a virgin. Christ was the "firstborn," the one who most perfectly belonged to God. By his death on the cross, the Christians claimed that he had opened man to the freedom of eternal life. Man would no longer be the prisoner of his own instincts and base desires, no longer the slave of his weak and "sinful" human flesh. For this reason, John the Baptist, in prophetic terms, called Jesus the "lamb of God who takes away the sins of the world."

The sacrifice of Christ, however, was said to be a final one, and it put an end to any kind of imperfect sacrifice. Thus it is written in the letter to the Hebrews:

> . . . according to the [Jewish] law almost anything has to be purified with blood; . . . Christ does not have to offer himself again and again, like the high priest going into the sanctuary year after year with the blood that is not his own. . . . Instead of that, he has made his appearance once and for all, now at the end of the last age, to do away with sin by sacrificing himself.

In the same letter the author said, "Bulls' blood and goats' blood are useless for taking away sins." And in writing to the Ephesians, Paul said, "Blessed be God the Father of our Lord Jesus Christ . . . in whom, through his blood, we gain our freedom, the forgiveness of our sins."

The Christian myth of salvation goes on to assert that man cannot be saved apart from the death of Christ. Not only is man born imperfect and in sin, but he commits numberless sins during his lifetime and constantly needs to be restored to the friendship of God. By himself, man is helpless because a

giant chasm stands between him and God. Through centuries of imperfect sacrifice, he could not bridge this chasm.
Then, Christ came. The "perfect sacrifice" had come, and
man would be saved by the shedding of his "Redeemer's"
blood.

To a Christian raised in the Jewish world of sacrifice, this
made some sense. To the Roman even, who had read the
legend of the consul Decius who plunged into the midst of
enemy forces as a heroic sacrifice to the gods, this might have
some meaning. To any man of the ancient world who stood
before God as a helpless victim, who believed himself a
hopeless sinner, who considered God an unapproachable and
angry judge, the sacrificial death of Christ was a myth of
some substance. But to modern man, it makes far less sense.
To me, it is a primitive "salvation" myth which portrays an
angry father appeased by the bloody death of his own son. It
is a primitive tale of unbelievable cruelty. It harks back to
the *Odyssey* of Homer: "But when with vows and prayers I
had made supplication to the tribes of the dead, I took the
sheep and cut their throats over the pit, and dark blood ran
forth." It sounds like a sacrifice to Rhea, the mother-goddess
in Greek mythology: "Son of Aeson, thou must climb to this
temple . . . and propitiate the mother of all the blessed
gods on her fair throne and the stormy blasts shall cease." It
sounds like the world of the ancient Persians: "I will sacrifice
unto Mithra, the lord of the wide pastures, who has a thousand ears, ten thousand eyes." But in modern life, the only
parallel would be some event similar to that of the psychotic
art student who killed a co-ed recently because he had been
"directed by God" to free her from evil spirits.

I accept the fact that Christ died, even that he was cruci-
fied. But I cannot accept the myth that his death was an

atonement for my sins. The salvation myth as it appears in the New Testament is an interpretation. It is a primitive myth, in essence parallel to the salvation myths of primitive peoples everywhere, but it is more unbelievable and cruel than most myths. It rings of a world in which man could appease the god of thunder during a storm. Now cats and dogs are frightened during storms; man stays inside and understands the natural phenomenon that is taking place.

Modern Christian theologians have come to realize that man finds it hard to accept the "salvation" myth. They have, of late, played down the crucifixion of Christ and emphasized his Resurrection. They have ceased, in most instances, to preach about the intense sufferings of Jesus and to make men guilty for the misery that they piled on their bleeding victim. They now claim that Christ is more a victorious saviour than a suffering one. They insist that in his Resurrection he made all men triumphant over sin and death. Thus, it is not the blood of Christ that saved men, as the New Testament openly asserts; rather, it is his entire life and chiefly his glorious Resurrection.

These theologians admit, in effect, that the authors of the New Testament misinterpret the death of Christ, that their emphasis on his bloody sufferings was an exaggeration, a myopic vision that stemmed from their Semitic concepts of atoning sacrifices. They proceed, then, to quote Paul when he insists that "Death is swallowed up in victory," and to soften his words when he says, "Christ died for our sins." Actually, they still pay homage to archaic myths, no matter how they refine them, when they speak of "salvation" at all. If I must pay homage to such a myth in order to be a Christian, then I am not a Christian at all.

I do not want to be "saved" or washed in anyone's blood.

What am I to be saved from? From my humanity, the body that is mine, the struggle of my own spirit? There are many things that Christ has to offer me: his concern for men, his indifference to material wealth, his honesty, his fearlessness in the face of opposition. I emulate his courage and admire his compassion for the suffering and the poor. He inspires me to get involved in my own world, and he helps to rouse me from my indifference to the injustice that enslaves the Negro and the neglect that oppresses the poor. He teaches me the value of the individual, the significance of a single human voice, the power of love. But he will not save me!

Nor will I accept this mythical God-the-demanding-Father Who could treat His own son Jesus in unfeeling justice and demand his death on the cross to pay for my sins. Nor is the myth more appealing because He brought His son gloriously from the tomb. I cannot love such a Father or even be grateful for such a son. I did not ask him to suffer for me or even want him to. This is the arrogant Father-God of myth, the God Who dares to ask me to be perfect even as He is. If He could send His son to Calvary, assuredly He could send me to "Hell." And for this I was to be grateful and to thank Him for my "salvation"!

At times man has had his doubts and has wanted to be free from the God of "salvation." But this God has had the massive support of history and giant institutions. He has called intellectuals into His service to build Him into a giant system. He has had mystics who turned Him into mystery beyond all question. He has had businessmen who surrounded Him with mighty monuments and made Him a part of the culture. He has had dedicated men and women who described Him to unsuspecting children and who frightened adults. He has controlled men by guilt and fear and sophistry.

The myth of "salvation" became an elaborate one. Paul insisted that the Christian shared in the death and resurrection of Jesus through the initiation rite of baptism. Thus in his letter to the Romans, he said,

> When we were baptized in Jesus Christ, we were baptized in his death; in other words . . . we went into the tomb with him and joined him in death, so that as Christ was raised from the dead by the Father's glory, we too might live a new life. . . . Our former selves have been crucified with him to destroy this sinful body and to free us from the slavery of sin.

The atoning death of Christ became a giant reservoir of "salvation" from which "sacred persons," called priests and ministers, could draw "saving" drops of blood to cleanse man. Once Moses could sprinkle the Jews with the blood of a young bull to make them pure. Now the Christian minister can pour water on a child's head and wash him from the "sin" of being born through the power of Christ's blood. The ritual of baptism, a pre-Christian form of purification, became the Christian initiation rite to replace the more primitive circumcision ceremony adopted by the Jews. The cleansing water "poured" into man the very spirit of Christ, the "Holy Spirit" Who dwells within a man and makes him acceptable to God.

Recently there has been renewed discussion about the value of infant baptism. Karl Barth, a noted Swiss theologian, long a believer in infant baptism, announced to the twentieth-century world that he found no support for infant baptism in the Scriptures. This reactivated an old argument. The pity is that Barth sees any need for baptism at all, that the whole ritual cannot be put in perspective as a primitive and archaic initiation rite. I can understand that man still baptizes his children because he has some regard for the ritual that admits them to the Christian tradition. I cannot understand a man who can take seriously an obsolete sacrament that claims to wash away his sins with the blood of Christ and provides him with the beginning of "salvation."

Gradually, in the course of Christian history, all of the religious rites were somehow related to the death of Christ. The priest was able to forgive sins in Confession because he had access through this ritual to the blood of Christ. The sacrament of marriage was said to give the couple special strength in their union because it united them in the blood of Christ. The oil of the last anointing is the oil made powerful by Christ's blood; bishops and priests derive their special consecration from the same blood. Even such a trivial sacrament like holy water, which men use to bless themselves, was somehow indirectly powered by the blood of Christ, and it commemorated the original baptism with water. Every prayer reached the throne of the Father-God because the blood of the Son had penetrated the "holy of holies" and had made man able to be in touch with God.

The Mass, especially, centered around the sacrificial death of Christ. It was no longer a meal shared by friends, the last supper that Jesus had while living on earth. It became the "unbloody sacrifice" of Christ on the cross, reenacting at every hour of the day, somewhere in the world, what took place on Calvary. There, man was permitted to eat the flesh and drink the blood of Christ in the ritual form of bread and wine.

Very important within the framework of the "salvation" myth was the notion that Christ had to be God, because only God could restore men to the friendship of the Father. Paul seemed to equate him with God when he said, "Grace and peace to you from God our Father and from the Lord Jesus Christ." At other times Paul seemed to deny this as when he spoke of "God the Father Who raised Jesus from the dead." Of the four Evangelists, John was the only one who seemed to indicate that Jesus was certainly God. In the prologue to his Gospel, writing some three generations after the death of Christ and using the language of contemporary philosophy, John referred to Christ as the "Word" who was "with God in the beginning" and who "was God."

After several centuries of theological quarrels, the Catholic position became that Jesus Christ is the unique "God-man" and in his very person he is "of the same substance as the Father." When such a dogma was accepted by the Catholic Church, it was easy to return to Scripture and to "discover" further references to the divinity of Christ. This doctrine lent support to the "salvation" myth since the God-man was human enough to suffer and divine enough to appease the Father-God. In a new way, he became the perfect victim in an elaborate myth.

The third person of the Trinity, the Holy Spirit, also entered the picture. He had a kind of twofold mission, one to enter the heart and soul of the man who had been "saved," and another to direct the work of "salvation" in the Church as a whole. By the death of Christ, the Holy Spirit was unleashed in the world to take his place in the souls of men who had been washed in Christ's blood. He was the Spirit who united the Father and the Son, and his presence in a human soul would unite man with the mysterious Trinity. He was foreshadowed in the Old Testament when the very first book of the Bible tells us that "the Spirit of

God hovered over the waters." He was the "Spirit of sincerity and truth" Who would give men wisdom and Who would guide the Pope and bishops in their leadership of the Church.

But no matter how complex the myth grew, no matter the subtleties that were added by the great minds of the Church, such as Augustine and Thomas Aquinas, man was still the helpless victim who could not be "saved" without the blood of Christ. He had to replenish the supply of the "Spirit" Who alone would enable him to love. When he was baptized, the Spirit came to him with abundant gifts. When he was confirmed, the Spirit brought him additional strength. When he confessed his serious sins, the Spirit could return to dwell in a soul purified in Christ's blood. He received the Spirit when he was married by a priest, when he was ordained to Holy Orders, when he was anointed with oil at the hour of his death.

But this Spirit was often petty and temperamental. He would not come if the words of baptism were not recited properly, if a marriage were performed without the permission of the Church, if the oil did not touch the flesh. He would not come if the priest did not say the absolving words, or if the bishop failed to recite the proper lines in an ordination. Protestants said he came in a way that was different from what the Catholics believed, and the Protestant concept of "salvation" was not as involved as that of the Catholics. For a time Catholics seemed to say that Protestants didn't have the "Spirit" and Protestants retorted that Catholics only had the empty spirit of Rome. But lately the Spirit has been more ecumenical and Catholics and Protestants have acknowledged His presence in each other's sects and in the souls of "sincere" unbelievers as well.

But I do not believe in this chameleon Spirit. I believe He is a way of man's giving credit to God for what he must do himself. He is a part of the "salvation" myth which makes man a helpless victim in a mythology of primitive content. I believe He is a historical gimmick that has forced men to cling to their separate sects and has made fearful men proud of their own righteousness. He is a way for man to blame his mistakes on something outside of himself, a way for churches to bully men into believing that "salvation" rests in their consecrated hands. I do not believe He assists the Pope and bishops in their decisions or that He brings "salvation" to men. It is the spirit of man that will bring "salvation."

Similarly, I do not believe in the divinity of Christ. Man turned Christ into God only to substantiate the myth of salvation.

There is another God in the Bible, another God Who does not deal in "salvation" or rituals or oils. He is the God Who trusts man, Who believes in him, Who warned against pettiness and legalism, Who cleared the temple of the merchants who made money from the sacrifices of the poor. He is the God Who is visible beyond the myth of "salvation" to which weak men reduced Him. He is the God I have learned to know since I threw my "salvation" to the wind.

And once a man has been freed from the "salvation" myth, he can also be freed from the traditional Christian attitude toward human pain. It is natural enough for a man who relied on a suffering Saviour to give "sacrificial" meaning to his own pain as well. Thus, Christianity produced an endless procession of self-made martyrs who were able to wallow gloriously in their personal suffering. Religious writers and spokesmen helped them to understand that they must "carry the cross" and "walk in the bloody footsteps of

Christ." Life was to be a "vale of tears," a "solemn life of exile," a place of "bitterness and tears."

Such preachers and their faithful followers could tolerate pain because they believed that they deserved it. They could explain wars as the anger of God, and they could work hard because it was only right for a "sinful" man to live by the "sweat of his brow." They had a pat answer for every human problem, answering every grieving human being with a mystical kind of interpretation of the "will of God." Only death would end their pain and bring them their "salvation."

But now there is another man who does not believe in "salvation." Neither does he find merit in needless human suffering. He believes in life and health and happiness. He knows that work is sometimes hard, but he is striving to create a society in which it will be easier and more fulfilling. He hopes the computer will free man from work that has made him seem like an unfeeling machine. He knows that children die at birth, that young and promising lives are ended before their time. But he will not pay homage to some archaic attitude that speaks of "atonement" and "salvation." He will learn from men everywhere; he will transplant hearts or remake kidneys, and struggle to end sickness, hunger, even war. He will not live in a marriage without meaning, but will end it and find a relationship that modern life teaches him is his right.

The suffering of the world is the suffering of his brothers. He cannot stand back and consider it with the detachment of the prophets of "salvation." He cannot classify men as "saved" or "unsaved," as "baptized" or "unbaptized," as "forgiven" or "unforgiven."

Perhaps there is a "salvation" that man needs, but it is not the "salvation" that comes from the mythological interpretation of Jesus' death. It is what man gives to man by caring. It is what was not possible as long as man believed that angry "Fathers" and "Holy Spirits" would have to grant him permission to be free and human. It is the "salvation" that is possible now that man can look beyond the narrowness of his own nation, his own church, his own family, his own "personal Saviour," and be a member of the global village.

Man alone can save man; man alone will save man. He will not rely on presidents who promise him peace and give him war, nor will he rely on parents who promise him family loyalty and give him bigotry, nor will he rely on priests who promise him "salvation" and give him prejudice and guilt. He will rely on himself. He will "save" the world, not in a year or in a decade, perhaps not in several generations, but he will "save" it in the new and smaller world which can look beyond "salvation myths" and see man.

# 6. THE
# MYTH OF MORALITY

One of the more obvious evidences of progress in man's struggle to become civilized is the evolution of moral codes. In the Middle East, in 1901, a copy of the Code of Hammurabi was found inscribed on a six-foot column of black stone. Hammurabi was an outstanding military commander and lawgiver who was the King of Babylon about four thousand years ago.

Justice in his day was often harsh and brutal. If a man was discovered looting his neighbor's property during a fire, he was to be thrown into the fire himself. The penalty for adultery was death, but if a woman felt she had been unjustly accused, she might clear herself by plunging into the sacred river. If she sank, she was convicted. There were laws governing inheritance, adoption, and the rights of holding property. Unjust accusations, always a problem in a primitive society, were treated savagely. And the so-called *lex talionis*, or law of retaliation, was strictly enforced. "If a man knocks the tooth out of a man of his own rank, they shall knock his tooth out." Or if a man caused the death of another man's daughter, his own daughter would be put to death. There were even times when a doctor's hand could be cut off if his patient died. The Code of Hammurabi, by our standards, was strict and even savage, but it provides us with great insight into the attitudes and problems of that ancient culture.

So does the law of the Jews. The more primitive a society, the more direct are its laws. The Jewish society, with its Ten Commandments and hundreds of lesser laws, was somewhat more sophisticated than that of Hammurabi, but far less refined and sensitive than our own. The Ten Commandments were the law of a tribal people who required clear-cut rules and strict justice to maintain some kind of unity and order. They reflect the problems that faced a newly formed nation wandering in the desert. The very substance of the laws dealt with many problems that do not concern us today. Thus idolatry was forbidden because the pursuit of false gods would lead the Jews to mingle with the other nations and to dissipate their own tribal spirit. Similarly, they were forbidden to take the name of God "in vain." There was a special reverence for God's name among the Jewish people. To give a person a name was in some way to have power over him. The God of the Jews, Yahweh, was not given His name by men, as were the gods of the pagans who "have eyes and see not" and "who have mouths and do not speak." Rather Yahweh revealed Himself to Moses as "I Am Who I Am." To the Jews he was the one, true God, and not a simple, tribal deity produced and named by men. In later years the name Yahweh was not even used in prayer, but was replaced by *Adonai* or **Elohim**.

The law of the sabbath rest, too, had special significance for the Jews. The very day itself was a sign of the treaty or covenant between Yahweh and His people. In the myth of creation, it was associated with the day on which God Himself rested. "The man who profanes it must be put to death."

Any man who did any work on that day was to be "outlawed from the people." And not only did man rest but his animals and his fields as well. This law, too, made sense in the simple existence of a primitive people whose life was uncomplicated enough to set aside a given day for rest, and whose faith was such that they could consider this day as consecrated to God.

The law demanding honor to parents was of unique significance to a wandering and often disgruntled people. The family was an important social unit in the tribe, and disrespect to parents could lead, ultimately, to an undermining of overall authority. "Anyone who strikes his father or mother must die." Murder, too, was a frequent problem in the tribal society. "Anyone who strikes a man and so causes his death, must die." The word of a man was important, and there was a special commandment covering unjust accusations. There was no time for trial, no time or capacity to comprehend motives. There was a special law forbidding theft, another forbidding adultery and the kind of jealousy that would lead to overt acts of greed and lust.

The very wording of the law and the detailed listing of the crimes tell us the quality of the people. A stolen ox was to be replaced by five more, a stolen sheep by four. Sexual intercourse with animals merited the death penalty. A "sorceress" was to be killed. There were laws demanding that the "first-fruits" of the field and flock belong to Yahweh, laws governing holy days and special feast days, tax laws, property laws, laws concerning the kinds of food to be eaten, laws declaring men and women "impure" for hygienic reasons, laws concerning menstruation and sexual defilement. And the people were warned that if they did not keep the laws, "I [Yahweh] will let wild beasts loose against you to make away with your children . . . I will send pestilence among

you . . . You shall eat the flesh of your own sons . . . I
will pile your corpses on the corpses of your idols. . . ."
There were no elaborate and sophisticated methods of crime
prevention and detection. Only the severity of the law and
the horror of immediate punishment could bend the stubborn wills and the fierce passions of a people strong enough
to survive for years in the desert and to build a mighty
nation.

Indeed the Ten Commandments are a high point in the
history of law, and they reflect the degree of sophistication
that the Jewish people had attained through their religious
genius. But at the time of Christ, the Jews had apparently
become a very legalistic people. A vast tradition of law had
grown up around the Ten Commandments and the numberless laws of the Book of Leviticus. Christ referred to the
religious parties of "scribes and pharisees" of his own day as
"hypocrites" and applied to them the words that God spoke
to the prophet Isaiah: "This people honors me only with lip-
service, while their hearts are far from me." He insisted that
they had put on the people an intolerable burden of law, and
he defied them when they objected to his works of mercy on
the sabbath, or when they questioned his disciples' failure to
observe the ritualistic traditions of cleansing after meals.

More than this he qualified and interpreted the Ten Commandments in his Sermon on the Mount. He said he did not
come to "abolish the Law" but to "complete" it. He did not
look to the ancient law of Moses as an unchanging monolith,
nor did he tolerate the human traditions that had grown up
to subvert the very purpose of the commandments. Finally
he summed up the whole of the law in two commandments
as the heart of the Old Testament: love of God and love of
neighbor. In fact, he insisted that the whole law of the Old

Testament could be contained in a single phrase: "You shall love your neighbor as yourself." While Christ thus saw nothing permanent about the Ten Commandments, his cultural spokesmen in later centuries transformed them into a sacred and permanent code.

As the law of a tribal people, the Ten Commandments reflect a variety of life that modern man finds hard to understand. While it is true they seem to safeguard some basic values that our culture shares with the more primitive and tribal ones, the laws that Yahweh is said to have entrusted to Moses have no binding force today. For modern man is not a violent tribesman; he will not resolve the complex problems of his personal conscience by simplistic principles of archaic law. Man often confuses *laws* with *values* and, when he does, he ends up a pharisee, a nit picker, an unbending legalist. Thus in our society it is considered wrong to "swear." Historically, "to swear" meant to invoke God's name, or the name of some heavenly patron, in support of truth. If a man "swore" that his statement was true, he said, in effect, that he was willing to have God witness the truth of his heart. To lie under such circumstances would be frightening to a man who believed that God might suddenly invade his life and strike him dead or blind him for his prevarication. In the course of time, "swearing" came to mean any use of God's name in a profane way. Swearing was further extended to include any word that the culture found unacceptable in conversation, especially crude words about sex or the toilet. After several centuries, man had acquired a vast number of taboo words and somehow they were said to violate the commandment forbidding the use of God's name in vain.

When such words appeared in novels, they were said to be "bold" and "frank," even though such phrases were often used in daily conversation. And most of the same words are "beeped" off television in the name of some "moral" code. Children are disciplined when they use these words. Men are often expected to clean up their language in the presence of women. This is not to say that I am not offended by an exceptionally vulgar use of language. It is only to say that my reaction has nothing to do with "religion" or God. When to use such language is a question of taste and social propriety, it is a matter of custom and breeding. I can share with the ancient Jew the *value* of proper language; I cannot share with him or with his puritanical commentators the *law* which forbids the use of God's name in vain.

Even the commandment forbidding adultery no longer applies. This is not to say that our society approves adultery. It is to say that the complexity of human love in today's world cannot be handled by a simple dictum. We share with the ancient Jews a *value* for human love and the marriage bond. Some of our modern laws, indeed, still reflect ancient tribal law, as did the divorce laws in New York State until recently, which permitted divorce only on the grounds of the "crime of adultery." But these are mere remnants of the past that have been reinforced in our society by the Puritan ethic. They do not reflect the thinking of modern man. We do not put adulterers to death. We are more concerned about human relationships and the kind of loyalty and honesty that can produce a personal commitment. Adultery is a private matter, not something for public legislation or tribal law. Sometimes adultery is meaningless, at other times it is cruel and tragic. Often it is a symptom of great immaturity and the incapacity of a man or a woman to have a deep and honest friendship. Or it can be a reflection of a kind of addiction to sex. But sometimes, too, it is the beginning of

great personal growth and the foundation of a friendship
which later blooms into a lasting relationship. In reality, to
say "Thou shalt not commit adultery" is to say nothing important to modern man.

The very idea of attempting to produce a responsible man
through law is ridiculous. Law only produces a careful man
and provides a framework for some sort of social order. Law,
of course, has its place, especially in protecting us from the
sick and uncontrollable members of our society. But law does
not hold a nation together. Men and women do. There is no
police force that could not be wiped out tomorrow by a
thorough and organized civil revolution if men and women
were not basically committed to peace and order.

It is not law that makes a loving and concerned human
being, and certainly not tribal law. There are thousands of
criminals who live within the law. We hear of the clever
ways of getting around income tax, the intricate ways of
cheating the public in sales. Frequently in our daily life we
are exposed to "legal" violations of basic human values.
Mechanics and repairmen sometimes replace parts that are
not defective. Dentists sometimes charge for X rays that are
not needed, doctors make extra money on nonessential tests
or on overpriced examinations. Almost every business has its
moneymaking gimmick that is strictly legal and strictly dishonest. In the ancient tribes it might have been enough to
say, "Thou shalt not steal"—or to cut off the arm of the
thief. Today we do not cut off the arms of thieves nor do we
produce honest men by law.

Modern society is too complex to be reached by the heavy-
handedness of ancient law. But religious leaders still attempt
it. For this reason, religious leaders are treated with a patronizing kind of posturing by sophisticated men. Clergymen

are too unreal to be taken as seriously as other men. There are cute little jokes about ministers gambling or priests playing golf on Sundays. There are droll stories about bishops who had a bit too much scotch or nuns who were seen sipping martinis on trains. Television interviews with "religious" personalities are most often cautious and polite, as if in open recognition of the naïveté of the religious society. Even the late-night shows, which are most often open to honest, adult discussions about life, generally taper off into polite amenities and discreet questions when "religious stars" are being quizzed. An actor can be quizzed about his personal life, but it is an affront to ask a clergyman about his, or to suggest to a Catholic bishop that his attitude toward divorce or birth control is the product of the Middle Ages. The religious official cannot be treated like other men because he is not like other men. He is the lawgiver, the symbol of tribal law in a society that has outgrown both his product and his approach. So he is treated with the deference that is offered to the old and senile or to the obviously neurotic.

Part of the reason that the moral focus of the religious institution centers on the Ten Commandments is the belief that law comes from God. Most religions maintain this, and even the more sophisticated religious philosophies, like those of Augustine and Aquinas, or of Calvin and Melanchthon, insist that the basis of the "natural law" is in the unchanging essence of God. I do not believe this. I believe that law comes from man, that it is always a reflection of his own attitude toward his culture. "Thou shalt not steal" reflects a man's own respect for his private property; "Thou shalt not commit adultery" reflects a man's own concern about losing his wife. There is no need for God to intervene and to impose His will on men through law. Law is from man, and one of the reasons that the religious institution has lost touch with the moral life of modern man is that it has not kept up with man's evolving understanding of the moral law. To point to commandments as coming from God, to speak of primitive "revelations" as if they were presently binding, is to speak in nonsense syllables to the man of today.

With their emphasis on law, religious institutions have produced a type of man who can be recognized in the counseling framework as distinct and different. There is a kind of "religious" syndrome that he brings with him when, for example, he approaches a marriage counselor. He has a variety of expectations and prejudices that make it difficult to work with him. He comes with a special sense of dependency. He has learned to believe that God will do things for him that other men have to do for themselves. In his dependency he has learned to make unreasonable demands on other men or to expect more of them than they can give. His counselor is expected to be on constant call; his wife should not treat him "this way" because he has kept all the rules that he imposed on himself for life. He listens to the counselor with great docility and attention, but manages to hear only what he wants to hear.

He is aware of his own great suffering and often considers himself a unique and almost "chosen" kind of martyr devoted to righteousness and the law. He believes that, regardless of what he does, "everything will work out for the best." He can say with a resigned smile that his pain will "make a better man" of him, though there is no sound basis for such an attitude. Often he sees no need to change his behavior, though he has learned to admit readily, perhaps too readily, his wrongs. He says that he has his "faults" while implying that they are not of much consequence when placed alongside of his virtues. He insists that he does "not want to hurt anyone," yet his intransigent devotion to law may well be destroying everyone who lives with him.

He has the highest of goals since he is not satisfied with anything short of perfection. His drive for perfection makes him feel guilty and dissatisfied because he never really believes he has done a good job. Generally he imposes these goals on others as well, yet does not recognize his own fierce intolerance. He is seldom extreme about anything except his devotion to the law. He lives in a world of blacks and whites, disciplines his emotions with rigor, and controls his anger so expertly that only a trained eye and ear can recognize his rage. He is so "kind" that it is hard to be angry with him, so "polite" that it is difficult to be "impatient," so "sincere" that it is hard to tell him the truth, so "right" that it is almost impossible to penetrate his "holy" defenses.

He is the man of the tribal code, the man who has turned complex moral issues into legal absolutes. He is impatient of weakness, patronizing when he thinks he is forgiving, interfering when he sees himself as fatherly. He does not face life as it is, only as he demands that it should be. He does not really see people, he only classifies them and puts them in files. His life is a simple one; his responsibility is clear and well defined. It is a tribal responsibility that is content to follow an institution blindly and to accept devotedly its laws. And from this loyalty, he expects everything.

He is the man who looks no farther than his own narrow version of the golden rule. It has become his favorite motto, and when he says it, it means not: "Do unto others as you would have them do unto you," but "Why don't other people treat me with the respect that my goodness deserves?" Or, "How can you expect any more of me when I have already given and suffered so much?" The golden rule is reduced to a legalistic measure that limits love. When applied in such a way, it subtly contains within itself a motive for good behavior. It means, "Treat me like I treat you" and becomes another version of "Virtue pays" or "Cast your bread upon the waters." It becomes a powerful philosophy of controlling men rather than loving them, and it does not tolerate honest anger and reasonable resentment. It says, "Be charitable" or "Be nice" when such behavior is artificial and false. It reminds me of all the "religious" smiles that hide contempt, the "charity" that is submerged hostility, the devotion to law that is disguised arrogance.

The golden rule cast in this sectarian framework is the motto of those who live on the surface of life. It is the text of the comfortable, the shibboleth of those in power. The golden rule as applied by the religious sects has not worked for the Negro. It kept him smiling in his slavery and docilely shining shoes. It has not worked for the laborer who fought for his living wage when he got tired of waiting for his employer to "do unto him." It has not worked for the Vietnamese, or the Jews, or the slum-dwellers in South America. The religious distortions of the golden rule have made of it a motto of inactivity, the chant of the high priests of the *status quo.*

Modern man wants more than a self-righteous version of the golden rule. He does not want the obsequious love of men who make of him a kind of investment in their personal search for "salvation." He wants honesty, not "charity"; he wants direct confrontation and genuine relationships, not the pompous niceties provided by those who claim to know what he wants before they talk to him and ask. Today's man does not need this deformed golden rule. Honesty is his way of life, "telling it like it is." He will not blindly "do unto others as he would have them do"; he will speak to others about what is in his heart. He will reveal the price of his involvement, the depths of his pain, the cost of his struggle, the hope of his heart, the vision of his soul, the strength of his love. He is not afraid to do more than he would have others do for him; he is not afraid to demand more of himself than any man would dare to ask. He will not reduce his love to rules.

Even now millions of men are "moral" without the churches. They learn their values from parents, from schools, from their involvement in life. They learn values from within their own heart. This is what the churches have failed to understand: that man's goodness comes from within himself. The best one can say of any law is that it represents a stage in man's development, and the tragedy is that religious institutions have enshrined it and made it permanent.

A new kind of brotherhood now reaches beyond nations and families and religious sects. It does not talk of adultery; it talks of a good human relationship and honest communication between husband and wife. It does not talk feebly of "charity"; it can talk of a love that is not afraid of anger, that does not hesitate to reveal its wounds. It does not talk of "stealing," instead it asks a man to come to grips with his view of material things; it asks a man to be responsible for his brothers who are poor and hungry. It does not impose itself on man through law; it believes instead that man's goodness comes from his own discovery of himself. The "moral" thing is the "human" thing, and the "good" man is the one who is most really and humanly himself. There are no "bad" men, only weak men searching for love. Today's world cannot deal with man in universal principles; it is bored with discussions about "situation" ethics versus "moral" absolutes. It knows that a man can only answer for himself; he can only be moral if he does honestly what he has to do. It realizes that man will have to make mistakes before he can know himself at all. It knows that "morality" is only mythology until a man senses his own responsibility for what he does, until he is aware of his own place in the lives of those he loves.

It is this awareness that has moved modern man to stop war. He cannot distinguish between his brothers no matter the color the flag under which they fight. It is this same awareness that promises to give the Negro his freedom. It is a morality beyond all commandments, a morality beyond all law. It is not, as its critics say, too undisciplined to observe the laws; it is rather too human to find them meaningful. The laws imposed by religious institutions are monuments erected to a man afraid to believe in himself. Today's man is too responsible to be bound by tribal law. Religious institutions ask conformity, docility, a dull response to an ancient view of the world. The new man is not afraid to dream, to move beyond all law into the freedom and responsibility of human love. It is not that his love is too self-centered for law; it is too real to have boundaries.

Now Hammurabi is dead; so are Moses and the great prophets. Jesus, too, has died. The Evangelists who applied his words to the problems of their day are dead. It is man alone who lives, searching his own heart for the honest answers to the moral issues of his own life. He has outgrown the Ten Commandments that once bound a tribal people into a nation. He has outgrown the centuries of Christian legalism that forbade a man to believe in himself. Now he has moved past the age of religious law into the era of personal responsibility. No longer can he ask God to make him human; nor can he blame Satanic forces of evil for his inhumanity. Now he has his own opportunity, beyond the moral myth, to establish that man can care enough to love his fellowman.

# 7. THE
# SEXUAL MYTH

Some months ago, a reporter for a national magazine called me and asked me to make a statement about the sexual revolution. I told him that I was not concerned with such a limited revolution, but rather with the broader struggle for man to be a person. He asked if I did not think that the clamor of priests to marry was part of a sexual revolt. I said "no," that it was an integral part of man's search to be himself. The reporter refused to understand, since my answers did not fit the preconceived thesis he had devised. He could see no farther than the greater sexual freedom in movies and literature, in beach parties and college life. This was not to him a symptom, a sign of a deeper and more significant revolt. So he dealt with bikinis and miniskirts, the decline of the Legion of Decency, and adultery in the suburbs. He gave us another hysterical article which established that man is rapidly going to the dogs.

Such a sexual emphasis on the current revolution is out of focus. Our society seems to make too much of sex because the Puritans are still doing our laundry. Modern man is struggling to put sex in human perspective, and he must shock a few tight-lipped matrons to do the job. It is the critics of modern society who lack sexual balance. The movie

*Blow-Up* should not shock us, rather we should be shocked by the Christian critics who called it immoral. Many of us today are finally coming to grips with our own sexuality after years of confusion and obsession. It is a previous society, with its whispers and prudishness, that made of sex a murky pre-occupation. Ours has given man a chance to discover what sexuality really means.

We are not satisfied with the sexual attitudes we inherited from the past. We are not satisfied with the women who knew so much about being mothers that they forgot to be wives. We are not satisfied with the thousands of couples who married in blind passion only to calm down and discover that they had no foundation for friendship or marriage. We are not satisfied with the dull relationships that endured for the sake of the children. We shrink from the "religious" women who held sex as a club over their husbands' heads and received "divine approval" for such blackmail. Nor do we accept the men who resorted to adultery or indifference.

Today, perhaps, we are confused, but such confusion is the sign of learning and progress. Man's search for a balanced sexuality is tied to his search for God. For a time, perhaps, he must flaunt his sex until he is unafraid to be himself. Then, gradually, he can learn his own uniqueness in the closeness of marital love. This closeness is what he seeks, this sense of being unique and special, this sense of being himself. This is what God is all about; this is the focus of Christ's love. Man, the unique animal, will know symbolically that divine love is the complete giving and surrender of sexual love.

Frequently I counsel men and women who know none of this. Recently a woman told me that her husband is happy as long as she goes through the motions of sexual love twice a week. Probably she does satisfy some physical need and leaves him a little less restless at his work. But she does not reach him at the core of his own loneliness where God must speak to man. There is nothing creative about her sexuality, nothing unique or sacred. She doles out her favors like a prostitute or a sex machine and thus soothes her conscience in her biweekly attendance at church. And the strange thing is that her husband does not seem terribly to mind. He gives to sex as little meaning as she does. He tabulates the encounters, times his orgasms, and measures his manliness by the quality of her physical response.

Frequently I see another kind of man who, in not understanding sex, will expect more of it than it can give. He is the one who must fantasize every little swaying hip that crosses his vision. Though married, he remains a drooler, a dreamer, a lifelong adolescent. If he is charming enough, he becomes the constant seducer, as does his female counterpart. If his mobility and income allows, he will engage in a series of futile affairs, hoping that each one in turn will quiet the restless appetite that no amount of sex will sate. Occasionally he learns from such encounters and then returns to find himself in the remains of his marriage. But more often than not, he continues to search, hoping that the next seduction will satisfy.

He is, perhaps, less likely to learn anything if his infidelity takes place in his head. He would learn more quickly how empty is his search if he were to experience the frustration of a fleeting encounter in some safe motel. He would have to make a decision, either to continue in the stifling narrowness of secret affairs, or to come to grips with his marriage and begin or end it. Frequently the churches and synagogues have helped to make of him a coward. They have pressured him to remain in a marriage that can lead nowhere. They hold his children over his head and make him feel guilty; or they promise him a meaningful heaven that will give fulfillment to a meaningless life. Or they tell shrunken men and frigid women how unsatisfying sex really is, so much have they divorced it from its genuine meaning.

Modern man will not stand for this. Even before he is married, he will likely know much about sex. He will not be an overeager boy on his honeymoon. Or if he is, he is taking a dangerous gamble that his marriage will last. This is not to say that there can be no happy marriage where virginity is a condition of the courtship. This is merely to say that marriage is an extreme gamble in any case. But whenever there is little more than sexual excitement bringing it about, the odds are almost impossible. And all too many marriages have been entered into to legalize the sex act.

Most modern men and women, however, want sexual experience before marriage so they will not be as naïve and disillusioned as, possibly, their parents were. Nietzsche was not far wrong when he said that many laws of morality were merely the resentment of one generation for the freedom and wisdom of another. I find this very often true in matters of sexuality—the frigid and frustrated impose rules on the young to make certain that they become equally unfulfilled and miserable.

The lack of sexual experience has been a major factor in our high rate of divorce. Our rigid rules of sex have forced many young people into a permanent marriage in the past. Today, youth is more apt to learn from a temporary relationship. The immediate presumption by the conservative moralist is that such temporary relationships must of necessity be irresponsible. Currently, however, there is abundant evidence to contradict this attitude. Premarital sex does not have to be promiscuous, and once a man has reached a certain degree of maturity, it seldom is. Traditionalists have difficulty in understanding this. The young man who admits to them his "sins" of premarital sex is told that he has committed a serious wrong. There is little or no attempt to discover if his act was irresponsible and self-indulgent, or a creative effort to produce that personal closeness and complete understanding that can lead to commitment.

Most of us have known promiscuity in some form or other, either in actual physical union or in the limitless world of fantasy. Few of us are so rigid and self-contained that our sexual frustrations have not been expressed in some obvious way. Yet many social critics are afraid to reflect on their own experience and to discover what it means. Modern man, in growing numbers, is not unwilling to reflect and to experiment. No matter what anyone thinks, premarital sex is a growing phenomenon in our society, and the modern parent or philosopher has to deal with it realistically or be classified as irrelevant.

They must know that modern man is reflecting on a problem much more profound than the sexual permissiveness that Puritan critics abhor. He is not preoccupied with sexual techniques or the right to engage in sex before marriage. More and more he takes these for granted. He is concerned with the kind of personal closeness and honest communication that makes marriage possible. Often he is not satisfied with the relationship that his parents had. He wants more. He does not want a job that leaves him little time for creative love; nor does he want a family so abundant that he and his wife have no chance to grow close. He will not remain in a dead marriage; no church or familial guilt will force him to sacrifice his dignity and chance for love. So he prepares for marriage by reflecting on the kind of relationship that can bring happiness and personal fulfillment.

So serious is he about marriage that I have heard him discuss openly his relationship in a counseling or therapy group. I have heard a young unmarried couple talk honestly in the presence of others about a sexual encounter they had a few nights before. The girl told how frightened she was, how tense and unfulfilled. The group was not easy on her. They suggested that she found it easier to have intercourse than to discuss with the young man how she felt. From the group he learned that he related to every woman only through physical sex and the pressure of his talented seduction. He discovered how simple it was to take a woman to bed, how difficult it was to reveal himself and to risk being rejected. This couple discovered how inhibited they were, how dishonest, how fearful of open communication, how ill prepared for marriage.

In such a group there was no talk of church morality. There was little attention paid to the simple fact of physical sex. But there was serious attention paid to the way in which two people used each other dishonestly. This was the most moral talk of all. The responsibility of one person to another could not be reduced to a simple act of confession or a guilty request for God's forgiveness. It had to be faced, to be dealt with, to be included in a man and woman's picture of self. In the past, such a couple might well have been pushed into marriage. It could have been disastrous. Now, in an atmosphere of freedom, they were able to discover how little they felt of the unique closeness that can lead to genuine love.

This is what man and woman want. Not the relief of physical tension alone, not a series of dishonest seductions that offer momentary comfort, but the sense of being one's true self in a fulfilling relationship—the sense of being loved in a unique and special way, of loving honestly amid frailty and confusion. Man and woman are not asking sex to deliver more than it can, but they expect sexual love to make a man know that he is the beloved of God because he is the beloved of another person. This is the revolution that is going on, not a sexual revolt to glorify nudity or to enshrine human orgasm. It is a revolution that will bring man through the sexual confusion of the past to the freedom of committed love.

Such a revolt will not occur without innocent victims. It may unsettle relatively sound marriages. It may give new opportunity to individuals who want nothing but lifelong dissipation and fleeting pleasure. It may wound the minds of the young whose parents have no love or understanding to give. It may break up homes that could have survived with counseling and patience. It may hurt deeply the naïve and innocent who trust too easily gracious words and empty promises. It may feed the sexual obsessions of the sick and immature and helpless. It may profit the lurid publishers who exploit the weakness of the unhealthy, but eventually such freedom and openness will produce much good. Man has never been so free before, and now he has the chance to discover what sexuality means even as some are injured in the throes of such freedom.

I cannot call this new freedom, however, a *sexual* revolution. It is much broader than that. It is the revolution in which man is so determined to be himself that he will trample on any taboo, no matter how sacred or seemingly righteous. Our sexual attitude is one such taboo. The Catholic Church enshrines it carefully with rules and definitions. Other religions, without the heavy legal hand of Rome, are equally as narrow in their attitudes and traditions. Society itself, without blaming its viewpoint on God or history, is likewise inhibited in matters of sex. The sexual sin is the primary target of curious and bitter tongues. It provides the ultimate in office and neighborhood gossip; it often ruins good reputations. Even the man whose own moral life is spattered with sexual affairs will suddenly become a pillar of righteousness in any theoretical discussion about sex.

It is difficult in our society to have an honest treatment of sexual matters except when we are dealing with the young. I know of more than one adult who has been carrying on a clandestine affair for years to be most vicious when dealing with the reputation of a young couple who are living together before marriage. As difficult as it is to discuss sexual matters openly in society at large, it is practically impossible within the religious framework. There adultery is condemned quite simplistically without any awareness that the very hypocrisy of religious attitudes has been most productive of such affairs. Frigidity has never been a sin, nor has the selfish squeamishness that has for some made sex a chore. Many a Catholic woman has been able to sanctify her sexual inadequacy under the banner of rhythm and self-denial. Other religious devotees have hidden under the protection of Puritan views toward the flesh.

Religious discussions of sex have most often been unworldly and unreal. I recently interviewed a married couple whose religious counseling experience was not atypical. They had been visiting a "religious" counselor for several months. He was a good and sensitive man, but they could not talk honestly to him about their sex life. It seemed indecent somehow. He was polite, made gentle references to sexual intimacies, but never got down to the basic feelings of the couple in bed. This particular couple had a genuine problem with sexual communication. They were having sexual intercourse far more frequently than either wanted it. Much of their sexual need was mere anxiety, the fear that he or she was being rejected by the other. Sex was perfunctory and unimaginative. They had never learned to talk comfortably about it. Unlike this situation, the unmarried couple having sexual experience will stay far away from the "religious" counselor when they want solid feedback on the state of their relationship. They know that the religious domain is not in touch with modern man's view of sex.

Modern society has determined that sex will be a creative part of a human relationship. Nothing that brings a man and woman closer together can be bad. And openness and honesty in matters of sex can be an important instrument in bringing this about. I have never had much patience with committees on censorship or programs for decent literature. Man must be his own censor and the tragedy of eroticism is not the fact of its existence, but that so many people are forced to indulge in it independently of a good relationship. Most of us learn soon enough that erotic literature or entertainment, even as any form of sexual self-gratification, is not satisfying. It may be a phase that a man has to go through, or pitiably, it may be a permanent state for an individual who finds no more satisfying form of sexuality. In any case, such literature has been a part of all cultures. It is reasonable to assume that it will continue. No committees will ever wipe it out.

It is much the same with prostitution. The best a realistic society could do would be to control it and make it hygienic. Our "religious" righteousness gives it over to the racketeers and forces a man to risk his life and health to indulge a momentary sexual need. Unfortunately, prostitution has its place. It is tragic enough that a man is forced to avail himself of such commercial sex. There is no need to satisfy society's pharisaism by making it illegal. So the girls hustle on the streets of Manhattan or Vienna, or they hail you on the way back to your hotel in Paris or Berlin. I used to work in a parish in Michigan that was in the heart of a red-light district. It was amusing to see men looking for the right girl without running into the police. I found it a ludicrous game in a sophisticated society. It was a simple failure to deal with man as he is, rather than as the churches and the Puritans would like him to be.

The strange thing is that we always blame our prudishness in sexual matters on the young. We protest that we must keep prostitutes away from our adolescent boys, that we must free drugstore racks from the kinds of magazines that will stimulate our innocent girls. We claim we are afraid to be honest about sexual matters lest the young overhear, and the new sexual freedom is called a threat to the love and beauty of youth. Yet it is my experience that the young have no great difficulty with sex if they are given a moral climate in which they are permitted to be open and honest. I hear them frequently discuss their doubts and misgivings about their sexual adequacy, the futility of promiscuity, the intimacy and closeness that are obscured by sex. They are not afraid of self-denial, and they do not seethe with uncontrollable desires for sexual gratification. Such caricatures are more often the projections of the middle-aged commentators who reveal their own frustrations through their advice to the young.

There are always the outspoken "rebels" on the fringe who use freedom of any kind as a mask for self-indulgence and irresponsible behavior. There are some "hippie colonies" that are composed of the inadequate looking for some concrete way to get even with overprotective parents. There are the college rebels who are not rebels at all, merely children who hide behind their student status. But beyond the extremists and the exhibitionists, there surges a mighty revolution for honesty and closeness, for deep personal friendship, for an open and realistic attitude toward sex. They will be heard despite the protests of their parents or pastors or political leaders. They will not accept double-talk, hollow rhetoric, or moral principles that do not make sense.

They do not worship sex; they strive to put it in a proper place. They do not see it as the reason for a marriage, but as a good thermometer of the kind of relationship that a man and woman have. They resent the twin beds of their parents, the almost sexless lives many of them adopted in late middle age. They resent the self-pity of their "overworked" mothers or the overinvolvement in business of their "important" fathers. They want to find themselves, and they know that such a task will demand a deep understanding of the mystery of sexuality. They want to experiment responsibly, and we who lead them and teach them must be honest enough to be of help.

There are millions of married people in our society who have a warped and distorted view of sex. They are not beyond help, but the churches have refused to deal with them in honest and open terms. These people are beginning to find themselves through modern literature on sexuality, in therapy or counseling groups, or in small groups of friends who will react honestly to each other. They are a part of the revolution to be persons and to discover the meaning of sex.

So are priests and nuns. Hundreds have left their religious

communities and thousands more will follow. Many of them, like myself, buried their sexuality or turned it into a defensive kind of zeal to promote their religious institution. They asked Christ or the liturgy or the dedication of their work to provide them with the fulfillment that can only come from personal love. Many of them, like myself, will marry and will begin to learn the meaning of giving and love. They will discover how vain and egotistical they have often been, how apart they have been from the realities of life. They know how to work, how to keep busy, but many of them will have difficulty in learning how to slow down enough to care and to be loved. They will learn about sexuality and discover that the celibacy they considered a self-denial was often a selfish insulation from personal love. At first, they will be confused by sex, as is any adolescent. Then they will begin to understand it and to know its beauty when it includes compassion and involved concern.

When I left the priesthood and later married, I received many encouraging letters and many hostile ones, each of them reflecting what life had taught my correspondents. Some hated me because my dedication as a priest seemed to give them some reason for the life of misery and bitterness they had known. Some warned me that I was expecting too much from marriage and discussed the experience that they had found in passing from illusion to reality. Some loved me and told me how beautiful was the joy of a happy marriage. A surprising number told of the meaninglessness of sex. They presumed I was leaving the priesthood for the kind of sexual freedom that a layman's life provides. They revealed more of themselves than they intended, because if sex means so little to them, it is because they have found so little of personal love.

Now I know something of sex myself. It is not as wild and

violent as my priestly fantasies imagined. It is not the endless
seduction that I foresaw in priestly adolescence. It is far
more. It is a chance to get close to the person I love more
than anyone else in the world. It is a chance most perfectly
to be myself, my moody self, my despondent self, my worried
self, my happy, joyous, serious, and boyish self. No act of sex
is the same. Each has its own meaning, its own special history, at times its own eloquence. It is a unique avenue to
intimacy, a precious road to union, a special opportunity to
possess and to be possessed. But most of all it is a unique
contact with God.

No wonder modern man will not fear sex or smother it in
taboos. How senseless to search for God in the Scriptures
and to ignore Him in the intimacy of human love. Fidelity
takes on a new meaning, the awareness that I can be so
unique and special that no one else will do. This is God's
kind of love, the kind of love that can make a human heart
know why it wants to live forever. It is hard to be sexual
without being close. Any little barrier is enough to prevent
proper fulfillment. Sex without closeness will not last. It is
asking too much of physical pleasure to have the permanence
that only love can give. Yet, the physical is important,
despite the sincerity of love. Even generous and well-meaning sex can grow dull. It must remain creative and alive no
matter what it takes.

Now I am a part of the revolution, and know that I can
continue to grow as a person, unique and special to another
human being, unique and special to God. Now I can ask
about my own sexuality, and speak of it, and experience it.
Now I can be involved in the mystery of human love, the
very special place of mystery where a man discovers God.

Now I better understand the tears of the woman who

came to me and told me that her husband had been unfaithful after eleven years. There was no way to comfort her, no way to bring her peace. With time she could hide the hurt, perhaps she would even stop referring to it in angry arguments. But more than likely, she would never forget. Something was lost. At the time I considered it hurt pride or humiliation. Now I think I understand a little better. She lost that sense of being unique and special to a spouse. Now I can hope, too, that by his compassion and concern, by a new degree of closeness, he may ease her pain and hold her in his love. For this is what life is all about, to find God in the unique and privileged love of man.

# 8. THE
# MYTH OF DEATH

I remember a sermon I gave one Sunday on death. I mingled the warnings of the Apocalypse (the Book of Revelation) and its burning pools of fire with the threats the Virgin Mary made at Fatima in Portugal to a shepherd girl. The church was as quiet as a sunset when I spoke. It was the late Mass which usually attracted the more alive and restless of the flock. But this day no one coughed or stirred. Assuredly no one slept.

I insisted that life has little meaning, that it is only important to be in God's friendship at the hour of death. I warned the man who was flirting with an "immoral" friendship that death would come upon him "like a thief in the night." I told the greedy businessman that his mounting income would not frighten away the angel of death. I described the final moment, the awful agony of a man who suddenly discovers that it is too late to repent. I described the instant awareness that all of life was but a preparation for the moment of death. I told of the horror of the guilty man gazing into the piercing eyes of Christ. I spoke of the impossibility of recourse, the despair of knowing that for a handful of pleasure or a moment's diversion a man would face an eternity of torment. I described the torment, the pain of fire, the loneliness and regret, the awesome and unthinkable reality that such misery would never end.

I could feel the fear mount within the walls of the church. I could see the revolving consciences of the weak, the worried and frightened adolescent, the scrupulous housewife. It seemed that I alone stood within the church without sin. I spoke of the availability of confession, of how easy it was for a man to be freed from his sins and to reform. And at the end of my sermon I spoke of the man who hoped that there would be a priest at the moment of death to forgive his sins and to send him to eternal peace. I described the man's vacillation, his foolish procrastination, then his sudden and unanticipated death.

The silence in the church was frightening when I concluded. During the remainder of the Mass the guilty were reflecting on their lives. After Mass more than twenty people asked if I would hear their confessions. During the week, I received calls from college students who promised to break up with their girl friends and from young married couples who resolved never again to practice birth control. I had frightened the congregation, terrified some of them, and the response indicated that my sermon had been effective. The "sinners" came to repent, not out of conviction or love, but to avoid an encounter with a sudden death that would drag them screaming into hell.

Once, not long ago, I would have shared their fear, and the priest would have been the most important person at my deathbed. I have been warned by numerous critics in recent months that I would be whining for a priest when it came my turn to die. An old lady in a bookstore told me this, a priest wrote it to me in a letter, a columnist said it in print. All insisted that I had given in to pride and lust until I no longer listened to God. I would grow more obstinate with time, and the moment that my soul left my body, I would face an angry and unyielding God. There would be no time left for mercy, only for the decree of justice that would sentence me to hell. There I would endure the physical torment of endless burning.

But now I no longer believe in hell. I am quite certain that I will not plead for the presence of a priest when it comes my turn to die. I, who once preached so violently of hell, do not believe in it. It is another one of the myths that man has fashioned in his effort to control man. It has worked with utter efficiency. Once it bound me and prevented me from being honest with myself. Sometimes it kept me awake at night as a child, more often as a man. It made me run to God in fear, scrutinizing my every act and intention, and denying the very humanity that came to me at birth. At times it made me calm and peaceful when I could say that I had carefully jumped all the hurdles that this angry God required. But then soon again the anguish would begin.

The fear of hell made life's joys seem of little consequence. The whole of life was gathered in death, wherein a gangster could find pardon and a just man could perish beneath a sudden and violent temptation. It was not important to do anything of consequence in life. One could be quite successful if he lived quietly without jeopardy or unnecessary risk. The best way to live, with such a view, is to avoid any occasion of sin. That sounds simple enough, except the occasions of sin are more often than not the occasions of opportunity and involvement. It makes for a cautious and fearful life, and provides a ready-made excuse for not facing up to oneself. Essentially, it is irresponsible.

Yet, if a man believes in the kind of hell that Protestant

and Catholic preachers have so vividly described, there is little wonder that he hesitates to take a chance. I have had hundreds tell me that the fear of hell has made it impossible for them to oppose their church. Everything human tells them that their church's view is simplistic or even wrong. And yet, they fear to move. They are not afraid of death alone. That fear would be violent enough. They fear the myth of hell, and like little children, alone in bed at night, they make of every shadow a witch, of every noise the sound of a dangerous intruder. Think of it, if perhaps you have never been brainwashed by this horror tale. You could be crossing a street or riding in a car, and suddenly, you are torn from time and are in eternity. You face an angry God Who will not listen to a thing you say. In an instant you are sentenced to eternal pain. You have heard hell described in sermons and have read about it in spiritual books. You have heard dramatic tales of men and women who compromised sin, and just when they thought everything in life was smooth and comfortable, they landed in a never-ending pool of fire.

Within such a framework, life is of little consequence, save to prepare a man for death. A marriage can fail, children can hate parents, a world can be at war, Negroes can march angrily in the streets, children in Asia can starve, the economy of a nation can be threatened, a best friend can be torn away. None of this really counts, only eternity matters, and man must do everything to escape hell.

There are millions who have been bound in misery by the myth of hell. I do not laugh, I weep, and I remember how hard it was for me to escape the sting of its wrath. It frightened me for years and kept me cowardly and hesitant. Now, thank God, that myth and misery are at an end. Recently, I was in a plane, and the turbulence was violent and extreme. We were forced to land several hundred miles from our destination. I am sure that everyone in the plane believed that death might well be at hand. A few years ago, I would have recited carefully my Act of Contrition. I probably would have announced that I was available to hear confessions in the forward cabin. But now, I made no pretense to pray. I was frightened, and I found myself wondering what lay beyond this life. I had no idea, nor have I now. I was really quite ready to take my fateful chance with the rest of men. I felt I had been honest and had done the best I could. I believe in the mysterious God Who gives meaning to my life. I cannot believe that I will be punished at my death.

I must confess, however, in that brief encounter with the possibility of death, I did not really think of God. I merely wondered. I have no clear picture of the world beyond as once I did. I do not accept the carefully refined rules of admission that once I preached. I do not pray for the dead, and I hope that no one will ever spend time praying for me. I have abandoned the mythology of death that was imposed on me—with its fires and devils and gnashing teeth—and have found no new one to take its place.

And yet I, like every man, somehow have to deal with death. I sense my weakness, the impatience of relentless time, the fact of death on every side. I read that a friend, a business associate, or even a stranger of my own age has died. For a moment I shudder at the thought that I, too, will die. Perhaps death is harder to deal with now than when I had the clear outlines of the Christian mythology of death. Then, at least, there were rules, hard and at times impossible, but always clear and definite. There was a way of dealing with death, a kind of *requiem* ritual that I could perform. I could appease the anger of God, pay my debts with prayer and sorrow, ease my guilt with ceremonial and tribal law. Now I am obliged to give up my idols and childish games and to face the reality of my own death.

Society is of little help. It has given death to the morbid undertakers who have learned their trade in the shadow of the church. They are as oily and unctuous as witch doctors; they play on people's guilt in new and sophisticated ways. They have made death into a kind of public parade, with their bronze caskets and limousines and private chapels of satin and saccharine. I detest their work and the mockery that it makes of death. Death in their trade becomes as artificial and vicious as the friendly atmosphere of one of Europe's tourist traps, or the phony glitter of our own Las Vegas. They are the paid vultures who hover over bodies and bury them in expensive plots before the living are able to decide anything for themselves. They have not improved the mythology of the churches. They have only borrowed it and made it worse. I would not give them my body, nor will any man a hundred years from now. I would rather my ashes ride the independent wind or my flesh feed the hungry fishes of the sea. I hope my friends will miss me, not pray for me, will long for my presence, not join the parade that professionals have planned to make money at my death. I hope they will comfort the few that loved me most.

Now I have no mythology of death, nothing but faith in the God of meaning that I somehow try to love. I believe that death is not the end of life, but I know little more than that. I cannot accept death as the end of everything. It makes no sense. It interrupts the order of life that I seem to experience. I see an old man who has struggled to find himself for seventy-five years. He has discovered the peace and beauty of life. He has mastered the man who once was restless and impatient, greedy and lonely, young and impulsive. His anger has cooled into tolerance and love. His wrinkles tell the story of a thousand struggles to give to loved ones and to wring meaning out of life. This man I see is not one of the disgruntled old, not miserable and selfish. He is loving, warm, talkative, reflective, and free. His eyes twinkle with a joy that a young man can never know, and they shine with a purity that only comes with the innocence of age. His smile is radiant and honest. His hand upon mine is warm and real. He does not boast or hide; he expresses in his whole being the wonder of a human life.

But soon he will die. I can accept the death of his body. I have watched it grow wearier with the years. But his spirit seemed to grow more youthful and free. I cannot believe this spirit will cease to exist. It does not represent an end, but a beginning. It needs to be freed from the body that struggled with it, that fought it, that gave it weariness and pain. But the spirit has won out; the man's eyes and inner beauty reveal that. For this reason I cannot believe that his life is at an end. I do not know what happens after death. I do not know if he will be transformed in new and responsive flesh. But I do not believe he passes from existence, not when his whole life was a journey to be free.

And in my own existence, I see my body grow a bit less vigorous even as my spirit grows a bit more free. And yet, I know death comes, and when it comes, I know it will find me more loving and fulfilled than I was the year before. The longer death waits, the greater the chance I have to become the kind of man I want to be, the kind of man I know I can be. If death ends my struggle, if there is nothing after death, then my quest for freedom of spirit would not make as much sense to me as it now does when I look at the world about me. I see all of creation, plants and animals, stars and space alike, gathered to serve and to challenge man, to aid him in his struggle for freedom and love. I see man as the interpreter of all creation, the healer, the searcher, the hopeful, the curious. I see man fail and abuse his dignity; I see him wound his fellowman and lose his vision. But I see him rise up again and struggle on to be the free and loving spirit that is his destiny.

I do not believe that the man I struggle to become will be reduced to nothingness. I can accept the gradual dissipation of my body, its quickening response to infirmity. The quieting of my physical powers only serves to simplify my life and make me find meaning in more essential and less distracting ways. With the passing years, I am less inclined to ask a new experience or travel to bring me happiness and peace. I know that I must become the person who is in possession of himself, the person who can be a friend, who can learn the joy and fulfillment that comes from love. And when I sense my growth and know that I am not the restless man that I once was, I will not believe that death crowns my life with nothingness. Somehow I believe in a life that endures forever, and I have no evidence but the power of my own experience with life and the experience of those whose vision matches mine.

I see and accept life's lesson, that as I lose my capacity to live with the fullness of my body, I gain the opportunity to live with the fullness of my spirit. And when I reach the point that my brain and body are too feeble to bear my spirit without senility, when I have reached the point that I am no longer useful to myself or to anyone else upon the earth, I do not want to be kept alive as some barely pulsating vegetable.

Even now I have no desire to be twenty again. I have learned the lessons that the twenties had to teach. Life means more now than it did then, even though my breath is not as even, my face is not as fair. I have learned something of the futility of money and fame, the enervation that comes from business and speed. I can accept life's pain without abundant alcohol, accept its opportunities and excitement without running in circles. I can let myself be loved and have learned somewhat to love. I do not have to have everyone like me, though I would prefer it, and I can accept the fact that I do not appeal to a large number of people. I do not make friends easily, but I need the friendship of a chosen few. I have learned to avoid the pressure of superficial social friendships, and I can avoid the parties and gatherings that only make me less myself. I can disagree with more dignity and less anger than I once could, and I can accept an opinion counter to my own with some semblance of openness and peace.

All of this my life has taught me, and yet I know how far I still must go. I know the shyness and fear that prevent me from growing closer to those I love. I know the impatience that makes of work an obsession rather than a joy. I know that I am too often preoccupied with trifles and miss the beauty that a sunset or a landscape was meant to give. I know the ambition that still pounds at my temples, the rising anger that restricts my freedom and makes my spirit narrow. I know moments of jealousy and self-pity, hours of discouragement and emotional fatigue. I know how often I demand that others be as I, how frequently I am insensitive to the needs of loved ones close at hand. And yet, I know that I will grow to the maturity of spirit and the fullness of heart that is my destiny as a person. I know because the past gives me courage, and at present, the future seems to give me time.

And yet, I do not know what lies beyond my death. I believe that somehow, I will continue to live. Yet, I cannot give evidence for my position, only an intuition. There is, as yet, no adequate evidence. And so I live my life, not in fear of death, but in the hope that I can become a person more loving and human. I believe that I am more than the dog or cat I love, more than the ducks and geese I have studied and admired. I am a man whose very words and breath can give hope and meaning to a few. I do not have to kill to show my anger, because someone cares and will listen. I do not have to strike out, because I know the power of someone's human love. My pain is of concern, my voice of significance, my presence a need. The longer I live, the more meaning, the less diversion, has my life. This speaks to me of an eternal life wherein I shall only fulfill the life that I have initiated here.

But this life counts, not like the Monopoly money that earns me heaven and rescues me from hell. It is my life, the life that I somehow believe will continue after death. It is here and now that a person is being made, a personality is being formed. Death will not terminate my work or blot it out. Neither will it repair the damage that I have done and give universal pardon or a blanket kind of peace. I will still have to live with my fears until love conquers them, live with dishonesty and pride until I can really be myself, live with occasional loneliness until I can be a better friend. I do not know what form I shall take, nor do I care. I do not know if I will have a body, though I would like to enjoy the pleasure that it gave to me in life. I only believe that I will continue to exist. I believe it only because the inner logic of my own spirit somehow reveals it to me. I believe it because I share what is to me the single most important intuition of Jesus Christ.

He is the prophet of a life after death. Many Jewish prophets were skeptical and offered little more than the preachers of evolution who describe immortality in terms of a species or a race. They spoke of a people that would continue and prosper no matter the ravages of time. They built a society that respected its forefathers and loved violently its children, but they made no clear and consistent assertion of an eternal life. Jesus, sharing the faith of the Jews who believed in an afterlife, did that, not by the glory of his Resurrection, but by the power of his own vision and his faith. I do not believe his body truly survived the grave. I do not see that his Resurrection as a physical fact is of much concern. It rings too much of magic and of myth. If he walked again after death, those who saw him would have no reason for any kind of faith. They would be faced with a fact that a man had survived death or with a fancy that their imagination had played an impossible trick. There would be nothing of faith.

There is, however, a place for faith. Jesus, the Jewish prophet, had a new vision inspired by the deep religious experience of his own life. His vision of love was hardly new, only a reformed and expanded version of what man had already heard. Nor was his vision of peace a new one; it was just reemphasized and made practical. But his vision of life after death was revolutionary in its impact, and it said in clear and unmistakable terms what the majority of the earlier prophets had only hinted at in shadow. I do not think he came back to astound his Apostles in some upper room.

After his death, I do not think that he spent forty days here on earth as some kind of spectral friend from a twilight zone. I believe he died and was buried and somehow entered a new life without appearing to anyone to support timid faith with fact. He preached the reality of an eternal life because he experienced within himself the purity of an undying spirit. No longer would his followers have to blanch or turn ashen in the face of death. No longer would they have to pay homage to the pagan superstitions surrounding human death. Even the Jews were not permitted to touch a corpse, a kind of concession to the pagan environment from which they were spawned. But from among the Jews came Jesus, who took the vague longings for an afterlife and the misty faith in an undying spirit which his culture accepted, and transformed them into a personal vision of life after death.

It is this vision that I share, this faith that I embrace. It is not a faith in Jesus, but a faith in his vision of life. The fact of death becomes the very spark of faith. Death confronts me and makes me ask myself: "What does life mean?" And from this frequent confrontation comes the human impetus to my faith. It is a faith that includes more than life after death. It makes of death a source of strength and not an avenue of weakness. Eternal life tells me that nothing on earth is more important than the power of love.

I did not experience this when I lived with the traditional religious mythology of the afterlife. Then I did not really think of death at all. I only imagined that I did. There were too many props, too many religious supports, too many theories that stood between me and my death. Now I live with a sense of death, and yet I live without the morbidity that such a sense of death can include. My thoughts of death are real and positive.

I think of death when I look at the ocean or when I ride on its waves in search of fish. I see the vast expanse of water and know that I came from this ocean through the wonder of evolution and the majesty of life. I am aware that I am a part of all of this, that the struggle of my own spirit to be free is the struggle of every living thing to survive. I have a sense of death when I see the grandeur of the mountains and know that the power of these formations are a fierce monument to the determination of nature and its human lord. I feel my death in all the fossilized forms that have died to give me life. I somehow know at moments like these that I am part of a seething, violent battle of reality to transform itself from mute beauty and revolving forms into the power of an ever more conscious, ever more free and loving spirit. It is then that I rejoice in my life with its new awareness of the strength of human love. It is then that I sense the very power of death as a kind of entrance to a new and more exhilarating kind of life. It is then that I see the futility of a life that is lived in search of an earthly paradise or for heavenly rewards.

My sense of death mocks the rich who hide behind their material symbols and squander their desire for immortality in marble monuments. It laughs at the man I met today who sees himself as exceptional and important because he has showered his wife and family with expensive trinkets. In reality he is a prisoner, as helpless as a mountain, built by forces he cannot control, and he has turned human love into emptiness and an expense account. He has kept his family at a respectful distance by enshrining his own success and by giving those who want to love him everything except his time and personal love. He pays for men to show him kindness in the most sophisticated clubs. He has everything but peace and joy and honest friends.

But my sense of death mocks, as well, the "religious" man who lives his life in the hope of some reward from the legendary god of the heavenly myth, and who lives his life in fear of an eternal hell. Such a man stands apart from life, he is not in the mainstream, and he is not ultimately responsible; there is always a way out. He does not have to be committed to love, to the struggle for the personal freedom that makes man truly human. He can be content to earn merit badges and to be rewarded by some eternal and omnipotent boy scout in the sky. He can hope for mercy at the hour of death; he can await some final liberation that turns him into the loving man he never became in life. He can stand apart from men, carefully tucked into his own mythology. He may never have to know the ultimate confrontation of the man who refuses to turn his fear and uncertainty into a hierarchy of gods and choir lofts. But he will never know his strength; he will never know his commitment to life. He will never know the power of his freedom and the depths of his love.

And when I listen to him tell about his vision of an afterlife, I am hard pressed to know whether I despise more his heaven or his hell. His hell, indeed, is awesome and resentful. It is the revenge that a child might seek against his playmates, revenge learned in a sudden burst of anger and fantasy. It is a native's superstition, a helpless savage's fear of a boiling volcano, a weak man's desperate threat to keep the strong in line. But his vision of heaven is, perhaps, more disturbing still. It is stuffy and effeminate, dull and meaningless, childish and superstitious. It is the promise of a finicky mother who will not let her children dirty themselves in the streets of life. It is the pledge of an old maid who makes a fetish of everything she fears, and who imposes her prudish rules on everyone she meets. It is a dull scene, an endless afternoon in grandma's parlor where the rewards are as meaningless as the punishments.

My vision of an afterlife is more like that of the man who does not believe in such a life at all, rather than that of the man of the religious myth. The man who does not believe in an afterlife can recognize and pity the artificial existence of the rich man I have described. Assuredly he recognizes the sterility of the religious myth. Often he is more involved in life than all the rest. Often he needs no convincing about the power of human love. I have numerous close friends who do not share my faith, who honestly believe that death is the end of every spark of their human life. Nevertheless they are in search of a life meaning and love. Even as I love them and respect their attitude, even as I reexamine my own position and compare it with theirs, I treasure the intuition that I have of a life after death.

I have no capacity to describe this life. I have no need to defend it, no eagerness to impose it on anyone else. I am well aware that in the future I may lose this intuition entirely. But presently I have it, and I believe that it enables me to put my life in better perspective than ever before. Not necessarily better than other men. But better than I ever could. I find it harder to ignore the sufferings of others; I cannot dismiss the hurts of my brothers in the world while I pursue my own "holiness." I cannot confess my "sins" or ask pardon of God; I cannot add up my virtues or clip my spiritual coupons. I am a part of this dynamic force called life; I am not its victim but its molding spirit. I have the capacity to love and to be loved and to share in the liberation of man. And when I love, really love, I somehow love forever.

I know my vision is vague. It can be no other way. I am
not dealing with physical phenomena or historic myths. I am
dealing with the distant depths of my own experience of the
meaning of my life. I believe that Christ's vision of eternal
life, when shorn of the myths that men have attached to it,
gives me additional strength to resist the emptiness of flattery and power, the prison of emptiness and greed. It tells
me that there is no power on earth that is immortal. Yet it
does not deny the meaning of life, the meaning of the
present moment, the impact of present responsibility. In fact
it highlights the present moment, because this is all I have of
life. It tells me that only love survives the grave; it says that
there are tragedies worse than starvation or poverty, more
terrible than war or murder or unloved children. It does not
make light of these, but it is conscious of the emptiness of a
life without meaning, the loneliness of a life without friends,
the bitterness of a marriage without love. These are tragedies
that do not need to be; they are not tragedies that make the
stomach ache with hunger, but they do shrivel the spirit and
desecrate the soul. Even as I ache for the injustice that
smothers the Negro or the misery that destroys life in Vietnam, I know greater pain in the tragedy of a life without
love. Such a life has no meaning at all.

I cannot say for certain that if I were to lose my faith in an
afterlife I would feel differently about life. I only think that I
would. Perhaps I would be equally as involved in life, equally
as determined to grow in love, equally as concerned with my
brothers in the global village. Perhaps I would be satisfied to
know that my efforts to do the best I could would help to
free the men who would live after I had passed from existence. Perhaps it would be enough to know that the only
immortality I have is in my children, in the creative force of

the love I tried to give. Perhaps this would be the most unselfish vision of all. But this is not my vision. This is not my faith. I believe that I will continue to live after death, and currently this gives great meaning to my life.

I have never known poverty or real hunger. Nor do I care to. I have never known the personal anguish and terror of my city under siege. But worse than even these must be a life without meaning, a life that could have been but was squandered for a fleshpot or for a surrender to power and prestige. To have had a chance to love, to grow, to know beauty and to have friends, and to throw all of this away for emptiness and gilded ashes is the greatest tragedy of all. It does not take wealth to suffer such a tragedy, sometimes a penny or a handful of praise and power will do. But it always takes pettiness and a narrow spirit, vanity and the inability to love.

So much of life is conditioning and cultivated taste. Once we thrilled to hamburgers, now we turn up our nose when the filet is a trifle overdone. Once we enjoyed a picnic, now a trip to Bermuda leaves us restless and bored. The rich long for the simplicity of the poor, the poor pine for the opportunity of the rich. The young need money, the old need energy and time. The salesman needs another customer, the executive needs another business. The poor man can't buy a deer rifle or a sport coat until next year, but neither can the rich man—so much of his money is tied up in property and stocks.

Christ offered a beginning answer in the power of love and in the victory of death. The churches turned his vision of death into a mythology that helped them to control men and make them frightened slaves. The morticians turned it into an expensive farce. The Great Society turns it into a dead-

line, toward which the empty must race to know every comfort and pleasure the economy provides. Christ turned it into
a sign of victory—man could learn to love before he spent an
eternity becoming the person he had begun on earth to be.
An empty man needs no fire to punish him for his lack of
love. It is punishment enough for him to have more time to
be himself, time to endure his own restlessness, time to love
when he has no capacity to give himself. Hopefully, eternity
will offer him an additional chance to learn.

In Christ's vision, life takes on new meaning; death is the
door of its victory or its defeat. Life's battles are of consequence, the battle to make a friend and to keep one. The
battle to win love and to give it, the battle to conquer vanity
and pride and selfishness, and to know the victory of a spirit
free enough to love.

Such a vision does not answer all the mysteries of life and
death. It does not tell us, as the mythologies attempted to
do, what is the significance of the death of a child, or what is
the meaning of a tragedy that snatches away a young life
before its time. It does not tell us where we will go or how we
will live or in what form we shall be. It does not assure us
that we will have communication beyond the grave, that we
will know again our loved ones. It is a feeble and incomplete
vision, a human and uncertain one. It stands before the
mystery of death with wonderment, but not with terror. It
faces death with a sense of expectancy and excitement, but
not with the religious fantasies that in reality forbid a man to
contemplate his death. My vision just is, I live with it, and I
can face the fact that it may be mythical and false. Presently
it gives me courage, it offers me strength, it provides me with
meaning and a sense of hope and victory.

Perhaps there is a new symbolism to replace the trappings

of death that have made a travesty of life. Perhaps the symbol of victory is the only one that Christ attempted to provide. Christ seemed to know how to live and to be a friend. He seemed to know the joy that accompanies such an experience. Money could not corrupt him, nor could prominence or power, nor could flattery or a more exotic loaf of bread. He could enjoy a vacation because he had a friend, and he could enjoy his work for the same reason. Death made him tremble, but it did not take away his life. It was not an end, but a beginning; not a tragedy, but a victory, an eternity to be the person that he had become.

I am not yet ready to die, but I am more ready than I was a year ago, because I am a little less greedy, a little less restless, a little less vain, a little more a friend. I need more time; I hope I get it. But I do not require time to rush to confess my sins and to receive the pardon of a patronizing priest. Nor do I require it to make atonement or to escape the fires of hell. I want it to be a better husband, a better brother, a better friend. I want more time to make sure that I can enjoy the simple beauty that is life, the everlasting wonder that is love. I want it to prove that neither money nor power nor vanity can make of me a fool. Such a struggle is not easy, and it takes time and reflection and honest friends to tell me what I am, and what I can become.

I need time to live my marriage. My wife has helped me to understand much that the priesthood was not able to teach. From her I have learned something of the difference between the freedom of love and the narrowness of overpossessiveness and control. I have learned what is love and what is merely self-consciousness and fear. She does not accede to my every demand, nor does she permit me to get away with the things that the priesthood so glibly allowed. I have a new and unaccustomed responsibility to care, to consider, to be concerned about the needs and feelings of another, who is as important as myself. I have a new chance to let myself be loved, to admit my weakness and loneliness and need. And to learn that in such an admission I am not less attractive but more loveable. I need time for all of this, time before the victory of death. I need time to listen to my friends, who lately have been able to deal with me more honestly than before.

Perhaps there will not be enough time for everything. I do not know. But I am not afraid. Perhaps death is the end of everything; perhaps there is no existence beyond the grave. I have no way of knowing, no way of proving my intuition that I will continue to live. All I have is a timid kind of faith, a gentle kind of hope. And if my intuition is wrong and merely another facet of the mythology to which I adhered in the past, then I will be happy enough to have lived with the beginning of freedom and to have been able to have loved.

Meanwhile I cling to my vision that death when it comes will in no way be defeat, even though its mystery will often be on my mind. Death, I believe, will be the door to a new kind of life, and when it comes, I think I will have had the time to be ready to spend eternity becoming the person I have begun on earth to be.

# 9. FROM MYTH
# TO MANHOOD

Even though we are in the midst of a religious revolution which is freeing man from the myths that held him captive, religions, on the surface, continue to thrive. New churches are being built, men and women are still preparing themselves for the Christian ministry, experimental liturgies are being worked out, thousands of babies are baptized, "new" Bibles are still being published.

And yet, a new generation is moving rapidly away from the religious mythology. Those who speak of religion's strength and renewal are the myopic and frightened. Pope Paul can sound as sure of himself as does our President when he insists that we must "respect our commitment" in Vietnam. Each sounds as certain as the university administrators who assert that the student riots and protests are born in immaturity, that they are filled with irresponsibility. All sound as confident as the white supremacists who shout that the Negro must take what he gets. They are not aware of the mighty avalanche that is in the process of "renewing the face of the earth."

The religious institution as we have known it is dead and so are its gods. But it is difficult for the man who took the religious myth seriously to escape it. One of my neighbors,

Frank, is getting old. We often talk about religion, but he finds it difficult to change. He looks back on a life that was made meaningful by the sacrifices he offered to God. When the budget was strained, when he worried about a house payment, when his job was in jeopardy or his children were sick or in trouble, he turned to God. Sunday was a special day of prayer, and morning and evening were times to ask God's blessing or to put oneself in His care. For years Frank survived an unhappy marriage by calling upon God. When his children turned out well, he attributed it to God's guidance. When Frank hears talk of the death of God, he is confused or deeply hurt. So we usually talk about other things because Frank and I are friends. Frank is happy and approaching the end of life. There is no need to unsettle the myth that has provided him with such important help.

The poor, too, do not know what to make of the death of God. Their life has been a physical struggle to get ahead, sometimes to stay alive. They are the Hindus who cling to their myths as they starve to death or hear their children cry for food. They are the South Americans who pray to the Virgin in their wayside shrines and wonder where their next meal is coming from. They are the Indians who live on beans and rice, who resist acculturation, and who bury their stillborn babies at the base of a cactus plant to guarantee another child. They are the miners in West Virginia who are trapped for five days in a sealed-off shaft and are brought to safety with the praise of God on their lips and a promise to be more devout. Such men must cling to their myths since life has been cruel and unreasonable and often without hope.

The uneducated, too, do not understand the critical discussions about Christ and the Church. They were never permitted to think about their religion or to reflect upon the

truths that they inherited from their parents. They learned
of Jesus through the religious institution and believe that the
Bible is beyond all question. Such people learned never to
challenge a teacher or a doctor, never to question an authority or to evaluate what they read. They hear secondhandedly
of a *Passover Plot*, a *Secular City*, an *Honest to God*, and
they are dismayed. The uneducated may be wealthy and successful in their jobs; they may be executives and salesmen
and the mothers of many children. But they know little
about history or the evolution of a religious institution.

How do you speak of this to a man who has no sense of
history? He does not know what you are talking about. He
looks at you and believes that you have rejected God. He can
only speak of what he learned as a boy, of what his parents
and religious teachers told him. He trusted them, and they
were often good to him. To speak to him of religious myths
is to assert that his friends were deceitful. He is the docile
victim of the Establishment. He views communism as a
monolithic monster that is waiting to wipe him from the face
of the earth. He believes that he must fight a war in Vietnam
to preserve freedom on the earth. He is proud when his son
joins the Marines. He listens to the President with unques-
tioned confidence. He believes that America is the same
country and that it is in the same world that he knew as a
small boy. And when he views religion, it arouses the same
kind of blind and unthinking loyalty.

But more than a lack of education, or poverty or old age, it
is *fear* that prevents a man from escaping the religious myth.
The fear is of many kinds, but at its root is the fear that life
has no meaning without the mythology of the institution's
God. It is a fear that resists information, that can ignore
facts, and overlook evidence. It can bind a theologian, a

college professor, a lawyer, a Pope, a traffic cop. The fearful still wait for the Pope's permission to be human. They are baptized to enter heaven; they confess their sins to find forgiveness, or pray to God in order that He will hear and change the rhythm of life. They look to the Church, the Bible, the past. They bless, they circumcise, they anoint, they look for "salvation."

Such fear is hard to deal with. It lurks everywhere. It keeps a nun in the convent when her service has lost its meaning. It forces a mother to have children she doesn't want even if she is losing her husband and tearing her marriage apart. It brings a man back to church even though its liturgy bores him and its sermons make him restless and angry. It makes parents feel guilty and unworthy unless they indoctrinate their children in the myths that were transmitted to them in their own childhood. It forces parents to cut off their own rebelling children and to live as self-pitying martyrs for their faith. It permits bishops to hide behind their office rather than to listen to men. It permits a priest or a rabbi to live in mental and emotional seclusion from the realities of the world.

I do not mock such faith, I pity it. I know how hard it is to escape. I have read men's letters by the thousands, begging, "Let me be free!" But they do not know what to do. For a time I thought the institution would help them. I thought that the Pope would hear the cries of the people, that priests and ministers, who saw beyond the myths, would rise up and tell the frightened people the truth. I thought bishops would be able to say, "We have not given you God but human traditions. We have no keys to heaven or hell; we cannot save you or set you free. We have none of the certainties that we once claimed to have. We are no different from you; we are only men who care about other men." The South American bishops seemed ready to say this at Vatican II, so did the bishops who had suffered from the Communist oppression, so did the bishops who had lived among the poor and starving. So did some of the Reform and Conservative rabbis who had lived with the narrowness and hostility of the Orthodox tradition. So did the ministers who had seen the Bible built into a savage and angry club to beat the little ones into line.

But then their fear took over. They did not trust man. They feared that his revolution would be too extreme, that his protests would be too dangerous and irresponsible. They were afraid to go to the very roots of Christianity or Judaism in promoting reform. Only the exceptional clergyman of any sect or denomination has stood up to be counted. They have not the courage, even when they have the enlightenment. They are afraid to abandon their myths, so they try to update them.

Catholics bring guitars to Mass and demand new hymns. The nuns fuss about their religious habits and the priests talk about a married clergy in the future. Reform rabbis travel to Israel and demand that the Orthodox give them equal status. Liberal Protestants water down their doctrines in the hope that the partial freedom they offer will keep men coming to church. But meanwhile Pope Paul grows more intransigent than ever. The World Council of Churches, despite its ethereal and meaningless discussions of poverty programs, continues to bicker about religious differences in a world that is rapidly abandoning dogma entirely. Liberal rabbis are afraid to pursue the course that their "reforms" should lead to: a faith beyond Judaism, beyond temples and traditions, to rest simply in *man*. Christian leaders fear to take the step that will lead them from "faith" in the historic system called Christianity to a genuine and substantial faith in the human person. The religions of the world are content to refurbish and modernize their myths.

One does not update a myth. One either lives with it and remains a religious child, or one abandons it and begins to be a man. But the institutions will not abandon their myths, not because they are stubborn, as I once thought, but because institutions are only people, and these people are afraid. The refusal of Rome to admit the divorced and re-married to membership is not the decision of the Vatican, but the terror of the very little man in the institution who fears that his life may have no meaning if Christianity is demythologized. So the priest clings to his celibacy, content to *wonder* about it; the virgin clings to her "purity," content to resent it; the faithful cling to their dogmas, content to profess "faith" in meaningless words. The Church is not the militaristic structure I once imagined, but a congregation of frightened men who fear that their house will come tumbling down and bury them.

The priest is afraid to look at his life and to admit that his service may have been largely pointless. The rabbi is afraid to take honest stock and to recognize that he has been promoting an archaic tradition. The minister fears to reexamine the "salvation" that he has offered men and to take a job that has some meaning. The faithful are afraid to reassess their life and to admit that they have wasted their time in the pursuit of mythological gods. To escape the myth would mean to them that they had spent energy in vain. The Catholic would be embarrassed because he spent years defending the Church's position on birth control and sex, and has walked out of parties when the Pope or the power of prayer was under fire. The Protestant would be chagrined because he has talked for years about the power of Jesus and the strength of Christian morality. The Jew would be humiliated because he has boasted for years about the cultural contributions that men made, not because they were men, but because they were Jews. All of the sects would lose the security blanket that gave meaning to their lives, status to their persecutions, support to their personal emptiness.

Even men who stand on the fringe of the religious institution, who have been hurt by it or who have been rejected by some official excommunication or spiritual death, are often afraid to let go of the myth. Lonely and discouraged priests, suffering people rejected by their family or parish, little people who have been made to feel that their lives are a failure, still ask that the Church approve them. They want the Pope to change the laws, they want priests to vindicate their wrongs, they want doctrines that hurt them to disappear.

Such a demand is only cowardice and fear. It is the Jews asking the Catholic Church to remove references to their people in the story of the Crucifixion. It is the Protestant asking the permission of the Catholic Church to marry a girl in his own church. It is the Catholic asking permission to receive the sacraments after a divorce and remarriage. It is man asking for an endorsement outside of himself, approval outside of his own heart and mind. Such approval is vain and useless. First a man must accept himself before he can belong to anything. Otherwise he is only living in a kind of dependency in which men and women lean on each other's loyalty to the system so they do not have to face their personal doubts and fears. Each priest or minister or rabbi who leaves his institution shocks its fearful members because he withdraws another voice from the mob, a voice that helped to make the mob sound mighty and fearless.

Even the bold reformers: the laymen who walk out of Church, ignore an "excommunication," or reject an archaic code of sins; the priests who challenge bishops and voice their protests before cheering liberals; the hierarchies that qualify papal statements and dilute papal authority by courageous documents; the theologians who face heresy trials and resist censorship—all of these are merely postponing their freedom. So are the reformed rabbis who confront the orthodox, so too the ministers who wrap their old doctrines in more attractive new wine skins. They are still taking the religious institution seriously, still treating its traditional forms and doctrines as if they deserved discussion and debate. They want the institution to agree with them, to tolerate their point of view, not realizing as clearly as do the frightened conservatives that the very essence of organized religion is under siege.

Perhaps it takes courage to challenge the Establishment, unquestionably it takes personal pain and long-endured outrage. Often the challenge is a respectable cloak under which the reformer can hide the depths of his total disillusionment with the Church. Protest can give meaning to membership in a Church that has lost its true reason for existing. But when the protest is over, there is actually nothing left of significance in the cultural relic, the religious institution.

The free man does not look to the Church for approval, he does not look to anyone save to the honesty of his own heart. If he has the courage to pursue his personal integrity no matter what it costs, no matter where it leads, and no longer to demand that the institution give him dignity before God and status among men, he will know the loneliness and joy of beginning freedom. He will have divested himself of the intellectual and emotional confinement of the religious myth.

Many priests and ministers cling to their churches because they need a job. I can understand them. It is hard to reenter the world when your training is in theology, when your advanced study is of no value in the workaday world. It is especially hard for a minister or rabbi who has children to support. It is hard for any man who has struggled for years to gain some prominence and prestige, to get a job that marks him as successful and hard-working. For such a man to fear unemployment is understandable, but I am saddened when such a man hides his real reasons for remaining in the religious institution and makes himself sound noble. Many priests cling to the religious institution because they fear their families; many people cling because they are afraid to disappoint their parents or a spouse. I can understand them, but I am saddened when they appear to rationalize their stand. I pity them because they do not know the power of their own dignity as honest men.

Many priests say that they remain within the organization to "reform" it. They say that a man who leaves the religious organization can no longer help it. He has lost his effectiveness. This is an arrogant position—to remain within the religious organization to "reform" it at the price of one's honesty. I mistrust such heroic reforms, whether they move a man to leave or to stay within the institution. I did not leave because I sought to "reform" the Church, or to be an "example" to anyone. I left because I could not be a part of a dishonest organization. I question the man who says he remains within to assist the Church in its renewal, or to serve the helpless men and women who have no place else to go. Men and women do not need his help. They only need honesty. They will survive without the self-designated heroes who sacrifice their integrity to assist them.

Nor does a man lose his "effectiveness" if he leaves the

religious institution out of honest conviction. A man has no genuine effectiveness short of his personal integrity. I believe the Catholic Church is a bad institution. I believe it cripples men and enslaves them; I believe it substitutes myths for reality and prevents men from reaching maturity and personal responsibility. I cannot be a part of it. It is doing harm to men, it creates bigotry and divisions among men, it prevents them from being brothers, it claims to be divine and infallible, it claims to be uniquely in possession of truth and "salvation."

Nor can I be a part of any church; they are all reflections of past mythologies that substitute fiction for truth. I do not believe that God made any special revelation to the Jews, nor that Judaism is any more than a historical development. I do not believe that it teaches anything of consequence that is not known to the rest of the world. I believe that its insistence on remaining a sect apart can only create new divisions and continued hostilities in the world. I cannot be proud that Freud or Einstein or dozens of great philosophers happened to be Jewish. I can only be proud that they were men.

Nor do the Christian sects attract me. They are only variations of the same theme: man's helplessness in the world. They only force him to look for strength outside himself; they only make permanent the boundaries that divide man from man. They are refinements of a more primitive mythology; they are palliatives that prevent man from facing up to life. I cannot be called a "Christian" because it would separate me from my brothers who are not of my faith. Nor would I be called a Jew in any religious sense, since it would segregate me from the rest of the world. I will be called nothing but a man, and that cuts me off from no one.

Thus I have little time for the "underground" church.

This is the half-brave effort of men who fear to take an honest and ultimate stand. As Protestants, they reject the Bible as a binding constitution. They question the need for worship, they resist traditional moral positions, and they abandon the Fundamentalist doctrines. As Catholics, they reject the authority of Rome and the bishops; they doubt the validity of the Mass and the sacraments, and they can accept divorce, birth control, even abortion. As Christians, they reject the divinity of Christ, and often even his role as unique teacher, as well as his place as Saviour. They dismiss the "sins" that have been codified, the ceremonies that have been ratified, the prayers that have formed in their churches. But they insist, despite their rejection of institutional religion, that they are an "underground" church.

Why are they a "church" at all? What do they ultimately agree on except their humanity and their attempt at honesty? Why must they be affiliated with the past? How do they differ from any group of men and women who, regardless of their background or their traditional faith, sit down together and try to be friends? Why must they mar their meetings with a eucharistic offering or a prayer service? Why can't they just have a cup of coffee or a beer and conversation? What magic is there in a liturgy of bread and wine that can't be created more spontaneously by an ordinary breakfast with friends? Why must they put their relationship in some framework; why must they reduce the magic of personal contact to some self-conscious formula? Why must they adhere to the ancient Christian forms rather than simply be together as men?

The whole current cry for "community" is often a fearful refusal to abandon the religious institutions. If man needs "community," as most men do, he will find it when he needs it. He will find it in a few friends, in a good marriage, in an intellectual or a social interest, in a neighborhood that has learned to care. He will not have to create it in some artificial liturgy or in some semiritualistic program. The man of the global village will learn to be a brother without the obstacles of religious frameworks. He will not have to know whether a man is Jewish or Christian, Catholic or Protestant, before he knows how to deal with him. He will know that he is human and that will be enough.

He will learn to distrust the word "community," not only the religious communities that he inherited or the "experimental" communities that propose to take their place, but the political and social communities as well. The very word contains within itself a contradiction that modern man detects. "Community," the Greek *koinonia*, the Latin *communitas*, centers in what man has in *common*. The Christian had his *koinonia* with other Christians, the Jew with Jews, the WASP with WASPs, the American with other Americans, and, of course, the white with whites. But the very sharing, the very "community" was an official act of segregation, and therein lies the contradiction. Man does not need such false communities any longer. They assert that he can only share his humanity with a few, with those of similar faith or background, when in reality he is one with the world. He is not alien to any man; he can find his "community" wherever he is. Racial and religious differences still exist, as do national ones, but they will have no substantial meaning in the future.

Political parties, for example, are obsolete communities. There are "hawks" and "doves," "conservatives" and "liberals" within each political camp. It well may make a difference which man is elected, but not which party. Political

parties are relics of "communities" which had meaning in a
world and in a time other than our own and are particularly
inane in our society except to provide two candidates from
which to choose. When Eugene McCarthy challenged President Johnson, he did not really challenge the party. He
merely reflected the party's disintegration. "Religious" devotion to a political party is dying with religious institutions.

And the struggle of the Negro is a dramatic symbol of the
destruction of past notions of "community." The Negro
knows that he has not been equal, that he has not had the
chance to be free. He also knows that freedom is his right,
and he is ready to dispel the myth of the white "community." He can never again rest until he is not a Negro but a
man. The Black Power advocates attempt to repeat the errors
of past "communities." They tell the Negro that he is an
Afro-American, that he should be proud that he is black, that
he does not need the whites. But they only produce self-
consciously another division. They cannot dismiss the white
man or ignore his help, not because he is white, not because
he is in power, but because he is a man. I am not proud that
I am white; I never think about it. Nor will the Negro of the
new world be proud that he is black. He will not think about
it once he is free from the bitterness that white men created
by enslaving him. There is no room for a white "community" or a black "community." The Negro and I can be proud
together that we are men.

Man will learn to find "community" wherever he is because he knows that he has something in "common" with
every other man. He may perhaps get involved in therapy
groups or in sensitivity groups to teach him more about himself, to teach him more about his relationships to other men.
But such cannot become a way of life, or they are merely
another form of church that separates man from other men,

that can eventually replace honest communication with posturing and dogma and a special language known only to the
initiates. In such cases they will only teach man to cling and
to remain dependent, to be comfortable with people who are
a part of his "group." They will only be a sect or a sophisticated kind of "underground" church.

The "underground" church will not reform the religious
institution. Nothing will. The religious institution is doomed
to die. The "underground" church will not replace it or
renew it. It is not doctrine that holds the Church together,
not law or faith, but the fear of men and women, lay and
clerical, to be themselves. It is the fear of facing life's uncertainty, of being confronted with the awesome, but ultimately strengthening, reality that life may not mean anything more than appears. It is the fear of having blind and
unsupported faith. This will not be changed by "outspoken"
rebels who are only heroic enough to speak within a safe
structure, albeit "underground." Such rebels will indeed be
applauded by the half-frightened sheep who stray with them.
But the man who has shed his myths, who has begun to live
honestly, will sense their cowardice.

This is not to say that "underground" churches are not
necessary. This is only to say that they are a kind of "halfway
house" for those too frightened to go it alone. They might
even be the good and essential houses that can help incipient
rebels to abandon the Church and enter the world. But when
they are all finished with their "reforms," they will have left
the Church. They will no longer be an "underground" church
at all; they will simply be an aboveground gathering of men
who recognize that they have more in common as men than
they have as Christians or Jews. They will not talk of Church
or even, perhaps, of community, but of people. They will not
talk of any law except love for one another and honest con-

cern. They might not talk at all; they might prefer to do something for their families and their country, for their poor, their sick, and their war-torn. Then they will have escaped the myth.

They will discover that the world already knows and approves the important values that Christians and Jews have set themselves apart as specialists to teach. The lasting truths that the prophets spoke are already heard in bars and in supermarkets and are read on "subway walls." The essential truth that Jesus taught is already known to children and their parents; it is already shouted from the housetops by men who never studied Christ. What separates Jew from Christian, Catholic from Protestant, is only what separates Russian from American, German from Frenchman, black from white, and white from black, man from man: prejudice, pettiness, greed, fear, lack of communication, ignorance, pride, painful memories. It is not dogma, not Jesus, not morality, not faith. Thus the religious institution, as a religious institution, has outlived its usefulness. Only man can help us now.

Jesus has been institutionalized long enough. Now he is ready to be what he really was—an inspiration for all men. His service is no longer uniquely the boon of Christians. The Jews speak of love as well as he does, and they practice it equally as well as those named "Christians." So do the Oriental sects, so do men and women who have never known the religious institution. Jesus is humble enough to stand in the background and let others do what he himself proposed to do. He is not looking for a credit line. He is honest enough to cease being a Saviour, an institution, a myth. It is the institution itself and its frightened members who are afraid to abandon the past and escape the myth.

For this reason I have no interest in ecumenism. It is
merely an exchange of myths, a swapping and a watering-
down of superstitions that should be abandoned. What does
it matter if an Episcopal bishop is consecrated in a Catholic
Church? Why is he consecrated at all? The whole act of
consecration or ordination is irrelevant. Bishops are of history, not of God. Man does not need them; they delay his
maturity, and they tie him to the outdated past. Nor does
man need priests. He needs direction and leadership in a
framework which permits him to discover himself. But he
does not need anointings or consecrations, whether they take
place in a church or in a synagogue or in a post office.

Thus I am not interested in Pope Paul's meeting with the
Archbishop of Canterbury or with the Orthodox Patriarch.
The doctrinal discussions of these men are well-meaning
anachronisms in the global village. These leaders cannot
speak for men as monarchs and dictators could in the past. If
after centuries of living together, after centuries of suffering
and war, bitterness and hatred, all they can do is talk and
gently qualify their myths, then I am not interested. Who
cares about virgin births or valid orders or saints and sins
except frightened children? Who cares if Mary was a virgin
or if she had ten more children? Who cares if Jesus rose from
the dead? Who cares if Jesus gave his Apostles keys or walking sticks? Who cares if he healed a blind man, walked on
water, or called bread and wine his own body and blood? I
don't. I care about men. I care about helping them, not
"saving" them. I care about feeding the hungry and provid-
ing the poor with jobs and helping the lonely to find meaning in life, and I care about ending war, not about redeeming
souls.

I will not waste my time with ecumenical discussions on

the nature of religious differences. Such differences are merely historical relics. What have we accomplished if Catholics join Baptists and Episcopalians, if Lutherans and Mormons hold united hands with members of the Church of Christ? Suppose all these religions are one. One what? One irrelevance that is binding man to a myth. By the time the religions of the world agree on their various doctrines, man will not care about such things. Man will be able to live with reality and uncertainty, to do the best he can and take life as it comes, without the support of the religious myths.

If the Pope and the Archbishop and the Patriarch are interested in man, let them stop talking about "faith" and the "Holy Spirit" and start building homes for the poor. Let them sell their art treasures to museums and help to provide food and jobs for the hungry of Rome and London and Istanbul. Man doesn't need another decree about "Progress in the World" or the "Credo of the People of God." He doesn't need wordy documents that only say in the end that Rome will always be the same intransigent dictator that it has ever been. He doesn't need Reform rabbis who are finally accepted in Jerusalem. He doesn't need a merging of churches and sects. He needs to know that he is the brother of every other man, and he needs to know it in some form more tangible than religious constitutions and papal encyclicals.

Let the Pope turn loose the ecclesiastical servants who prepare unread documents and rearrange archives and preserve outmoded protocol. Let him free them to work among the poor. Then when he makes a statement on war or peace or nuclear arms, it may sound like something other than a commercial fitting his historic role. Let the bishops stop building cathedrals and other useless monuments. Let them lead men in practical love and join the rest of the world to discover if life means anything. Let pulpits disappear and let priests and ministers begin to communicate with men. Let them cease being a Church and begin to be a society. Once Jesus made the test of discipleship: "Go sell what you have and give to the poor." When did the test become loyalty to petty dogmas and fidelity to ancient traditions? Once the prophets demanded aid to the poor and comfort to the dispossessed. When did Judaism become the preservation of ancient irrelevance or social groups determined to perpetuate themselves?

But the religious institutions will not change significantly; they are afraid to do anything but rearrange their myths. A few bishops will pour out money to the poor even as they strive to preserve their historic institution. A few religious leaders will join hands with alien creeds and attempt a meaningless merger. But the power structure of the institutions will not change. Rome and one of its cardinals will quarrel about the behavior of nuns, while in Southeast Asia the children search in rubble for their homes. The Baptists will quarrel about the virgin birth while the poor of the world are raped by the rich. Churches will build new buildings while Negro babies are bitten by rats. The churches will continue to baptize and circumcise and wonder why there are fewer and fewer men in attendance at their services. In some way, this is a tragedy, because religious institutions could be of great service to men if they could abandon their myths and forget their histories.

But they cannot. They will lose more and more of their leaders, more and more of their members. Eventually they will largely cease to be, and I am committed to assist in their demise. Religious institutions are evil; they stand in man's way, they are dishonest, they cling to myths that are not true. They are not harmless like a social club. They are dangerous like a propaganda machine. They have weakened man, delayed his growth, severed him from his brother. They have built walls between men and called them "revealed" truths; they have taught distrust and self-righteousness and called it morality. They have taught men that they are evil, that they are better than other men, that "salvation" comes from forces outside of man's concern for his fellowmen.

The religions have had their chance to turn the words of Jesus and the prophets into reality. But they have only taught the German to hate the Jew, the Jew to hate the Arab, the American to hate the Communist, the Protestant to distrust the Catholic, the Catholic to stand apart from the rest of men. They have prayed for the world while distrusting its science, criticizing its progress, calling it "immoral," questioning its sincerity, mocking its commitment. They have called its men ruthless and faithless, greedy and proud, ambitious and contemptuous.

The man of the global village will have no time for them. He has no regard for sects or nationalities, no time for boundaries or divisions. He has no faith in the artificial communities that join men together to separate them from other men. He is not a stranger to any man, black or white, American or Russian, Jew or gentile. He is less and less afraid to abandon the religious institution and its mythology. In fact he has already begun to lay it aside. He cannot respect a synagogue that makes him feel like a stranger because he is not Jewish, a Church that has little to say to him because he is not Catholic or Protestant. He will not wave flags or salute crosses or honor religious stars. He will only strive to know his brother, to be one with him.

Meanwhile the religious institutions will provide a comfortable home for the men and women who are afraid of life, who need the artificial myths to give substance to their lives, who need its framework to provide them with a job or a prestigious position. But the man of the global village will reach these people soon, or reach their sons and daughters, and help them to realize that man is strong enough to live by himself. Then men will leave the Church, as they are leaving it now, even the "underground" church, and find themselves as men with other men.

God is not in the religious institution. He is in the men and women who believe in other men. My friend Gene is Jewish. He abandoned the synagogue about two days after his Bar Mitzvah. He has no feelings about sin or an afterlife. He never prays. The world of institutional religion is no more real to him than the struggle of Atlas to uphold the world. But he cares about the poor, the ignorant, the helpless. Whenever I talk to him he has taken another family under his wing, helped a man to find a job, found a school for a retarded child. He is not Jewish to me, nor am I Catholic or Christian or a "former priest" to him. We are just men, friends, brothers, fellow members of a global village. He would rather give one family hope than update a hundred liturgies. So would I. He would rather get one man a job or teach his wife to read, than "save" a thousand souls. So would I.

Now I am living without the religious myths to which I once gave total allegiance. I have left the Church and I flounder on my own. But I flounder with a freedom that makes the struggle worthwhile. I can see life and death in a dimension that makes me feel a part of the world.

Not long ago a close friend of mine died. He was only fifty-seven. I went to see his body and to hear the Rosary recited by his friends. I found it hard to believe that three years ago I would have led the Rosary and would have asked God to grant my friend eternal rest. I would have said Mass for him and blessed his body with the traditional holy water and incense. I would have prayed that he might not have to spend a long time in purgatory. I would have offered his widow the comfort that he would live in peace with God.

But now I could only think of the last time we talked. I could only be sad and wonder where he was. I could not say the Rosary; it made no sense. I could not attend the funeral and hear the myths that gave me no comfort. I could not tell the family anything except that I was sad. I had nothing to lean on except my grief, nothing to save me from the reality that I, too, must die. So I lived with my grief, my uncertainty, my fear, and somehow I knew a little more clearly that life must mean something at the present moment. And in the midst of my sadness I felt a kind of strength that my past idolatry had never provided. I was glad that I was not a priest with a prayerbook full of answers and a sermon full of platitudes. I was glad that I was a man who could only be sad and wonder about life and death.

And as I looked around and saw the sincerity of the people saying the Rosary for my friend, I knew that the myth would not die easily, but I knew that it would die soon. The sound of the beads was the death rattle of an ancient and archaic institution. I was glad that I was not a priest, that I had escaped from the myth. I was glad that I could only look at the body of my friend and know that I had loved him, glad that I had nothing to give but my friendship and my sadness.

# 10. THE
# BIRTH OF GOD

There are moments when I find it hard to be concerned about the war in Vietnam, when I can ignore the trials of the Negro and the effects of LSD on the young. There are moments when I am scarcely concerned about the Czechs' struggle with the Russians or the war against poverty. I do not like these moments; I merely acknowledge their existence. When they occur, I seldom read the paper or recognize another man's problem. I retreat within myself and escape from even my closest friend. I hardly care about the starving children, the horror of life in the inner city, the scars of napalm, or the rising crime rate in our streets. All of my attention and energy is focused on me. I cannot get away from myself.

At times like these I am aware of how fiercely I want to live. I am fighting for my own existence. Sometimes these moments occur when I am struggling with my job or my marriage, when I am forced to wonder if life is anything but a complicated game. Or they happen when I am worried about my health, when I feel incapable of writing, when words seem inadequate. At such moments I find it hard to sleep, and when I doze off my imagination is sometimes filled with disconnected pictures that frighten me. I am forced to wonder if I have been honest with others, if I am capable of having a friend, if I am destined to be lonely and distressed.

It is then that I concentrate all of my energies on my own life. It would do no good to tell me to help the poor, to urge me to realize how much better off I am than the man who is dying of cancer, than the boy who lies bleeding on a battle-field or in a rice paddy. A weariness comes over me, or a fear, or an impulsive urge to run away and be by myself. At a moment like this, my wife cannot help; I can find no comfort in my work, and I can find no inner reserve of confidence. I am brought face to face with the feebleness of my own existence. Prayer does not help me, nor entertainment, even alcohol would not let me escape.

I think I would feel this way if I were a husband in Vietnam and my wife and children were murdered by mortar shells. I would not care about the war in Vietnam or the free world's struggle with the Communists. I would only care about my family and I would wonder if life had any further meaning. I think I would feel this way if I were a Negro in a rat-infested tenement. I would not care about the race problem; I would only want food and shelter and protection for my children. I would feel this way if my wife had left me, or if I could not hold a job. I would feel this way if I were told that I only had a few weeks to live.

I would feel what I sometimes feel even now—and almost without reason—that I am all alone. I recognize that ultimately I am an individual, and I must bear the burden of being one. I cannot really lean on anyone else. This is not to say that I cannot love, that I cannot trust, that I cannot reach out. It is only to say that at times I am thrust back upon my own aloneness, and I cannot appreciate my union with the world. It is not that there is no one to reach out to me, it is, rather, that I do not want to be reached, or I cannot be.

Once I dreaded such moments and poured out my heart in prayer. I fell on my knees and begged God for deliverance. I joined with Christ in his agony, with the tragic figures of history in a kind of personal anguish. Now I do not pray or beg for deliverance. I accept such moments as enriching and strengthening, as a kind of personal surgery in which my own identity is excised from accumulated artifice. I am certain that I do not suffer as much as many men, but when I suffer, it seems to be as much as I can bear. I know that I have not been tested ultimately, that some greater trial lies ahead, that even now, someone is suffering an agony that would tear out my heart. But it is at this moment of personal pain, this time of existential anguish, that I am confronted with my own crisis of faith. It is not a crisis that asks me to embrace doctrine or moral teachings. It is deeper than that. It is the crisis that confronts me with my own aloneness and asks if life has any meaning, if all of existence is not a cruel kind of survival.

I would like to be able to say that it takes a real tragedy to expose this weak and wounded side of myself, that it appears only at rare and important intervals. But this is not true. Usually I can survive my share of real tragedy with comparative ease, but a mere trifle in any objective sense can tear at my being. A difficulty at work, a conflict with a friend, a financial burden I did not anticipate, a gloomy day can sometimes trigger a disproportionate anguish. My whole being is rocked, and I have little capacity to care for anyone except myself. I am obliged to face myself in my human loneliness.

A psychologist might attribute intelligent interpretations

to my moods, but I really would find his remarks superficial. A behaviorist might speak of a chemical imbalance, but I would consider his suggestion irrelevant. A religious counselor might offer me reflections on the meaning of life from his well-worn mythology, but he would not hold my interest. An acquaintance might recommend a vacation or a calculated distraction, but I would reject his offer. I consider such moments as special times of spiritual growth. I do not want to dismiss them, to run from them, to interpret them away, to dilute them by some well-meant cliché. I want to live with them, to learn through them, to face the fact of my own individuality.

I refuse to force myself out of this mood, although I am often obliged to hide it and to pretend that it does not exist. Usually it does not last long, but I cannot predict its coming or going, its duration or violence. I only know that when it comes and while it stays I am confronted with the meaning of life. It can come when life is seemingly careless and trouble-free. It can come not merely when I am a failure, but even when I feel the flush of success. It only began to come with any degree of intensity when I abandoned the mythology of my Church, when I refused to live with religious placebos and palliatives.

Perhaps in former years I crowded it out, or perhaps I would not let it come to the surface amid the pressure of hard work and pressing responsibilities. More than likely I simply called it a "cross" and refused to look at it. I did not have to face this mood; I only had to be rid of it. So I lost it amid my academic dogmas and my structured rituals, or I dissolved it in the religious fantasies I had learned in childhood. Now I face it and ponder seriously the meaning of my life.

When it comes, I usually sit on my porch and look at the ocean. I reflect upon the meaning of my own existence. I do not anticipate a future happiness; I do not predict a life full of emotional enrichment and success. I just permit my own manhood to come to the surface of my consciousness. I am absorbed with myself. I resist the compulsion to do something; I also resist the inclination, nurtured in the religious retreats of my past, to figure something out. I just let my own loneliness happen. And somehow I am in touch with God.

I do not mean the God of religious tradition. I do not mean Christ, or the bearded Jew whom Catholics consider God or some loving Trinity that religious writers describe. I cannot reduce my God to personal dimensions, nor do I want to. I cannot contain Him in any kind of an image. Perhaps He is the Life-force of the world, the Unity of all creation, the pervading Spirit of all existence. But, to me, these are just words. I can only grasp my God as a kind of meaning in my life. He, and I hesitate to call Him "He," lives at the very root of my own loneliness and somehow makes my life intelligible. I am a part of something important; I am of consequence, because God is. I am one with the world, a part of life, capable of knowledge and love and pain because God is.

When men ask me about Him, I am at a loss for words. I hesitate to speak of Him lest I lose Him in syllables and in weak symbols. When religious sects try to corner Him or to reduce Him to their human categories, I know that they are telling me more about themselves and their needs than about my God. My God understands all, forgives all, loves me with an unconditional love. He does not have to save me because there is nothing to save me from. He does not redeem me because I am not up for redemption. He loves me and some-how I love Him. He is my life shorn of superficiality and phoniness. He is at the center of my being, at the core of my aloneness, at the root of my genuine existence.

He does not want credit or gratitude. He does not want a "thank you" before I eat or a meditation on His goodness when I am enjoying myself. I do not think about God when I am enjoying myself because I am not searching for mean-ing. I have already found it at such times. I do not think about God when I am playing golf or diving for a fish, when I am laughing with my wife or enjoying a meal or walking joyously on the beach. I do not think of Him when the pelicans are searching for fish, or when I am camping in the mountains or on the desert. I think of life and love, and I treasure the moment that makes me content. To me, it would be rude and artificial to turn to God and thank Him for my happiness, to pause and share with Him my joy. I am already in touch with God because I am in touch with the meaning of my existence. It would be self-conscious to turn aside and to separate myself from God, to sever my implicit contact, to lose my spontaneous absorption in reality.

My God does not want an expression of sorrow when I have offended my wife or hurt my friend, nor does He want a litany of repentance when I am faced with my own human weakness. My God wants me to live, to find meaning, to make each day matter, to struggle against the emptiness and boredom, the frustration and self-pity that can suck out all of my life. I do not have to worship God; I only have to find some purpose in my daily existence, even if that purpose is just to *be*. My God asks nothing of me because He loves me, and He permits me to know that I count. He does not invade my existence to remind me of my responsibilities; my own conscience can do that. He does not demand that I change before He offers me His love. This would be a selfish and manipulating God formed by men. He does not demand my homage. This would be an egotistical and controlling God created by men who want to rule in His place. He does not demand that I believe in Him, that I trust Him. This would be an insensitive and frightened God fashioned by theologians who have no confidence in themselves. My God *is*, and He lets me *be*, and in such a relationship there is the essence of love and the fullness of faith.

It is not difficult for me to play a kind of game and to reduce God to the pictures I inherited in my religious tradition. I can rehearse the deep-rooted suggestions of my religious training and call God "omnipotent" or "everlasting" or "omniscient." But when I have said such words, I have said nothing. I can speak of the relationships between members of the Trinity, the prerogatives of Father, Son, and Holy Spirit; I can speculate about the power and influence of God upon the earth. But when I have finished with my verbalizing, I have achieved nothing of value. I can turn my God into freedom from personal responsibility. I can ask Him to do things that I must do myself; I can make of Him an all-powerful leprechaun or an avenging angel. I can reduce Him to the level of a human friend; I can make of Him an extension of my own hopes or desires or resentments. I can transform Him into the essence of fatherhood or motherhood; I can depict Him as a kind of overseeing superman. But my God is none of these. He is the intangible, elusive, fleeting meaning of my life.

I do not ask my God for anything. I go to the men and women who love me instead. If, from habit, I ask Him for peace in the midst of my struggle, I am not really asking at all. I am merely admitting that I need something beyond my present, feeble strength. I do not expect Him to come rushing to my aid with some "supernatural" power. I do not expect Him to come at all. I only want to be aware of Him, to know that my life means something. I merely want to be aware of His presence since at times I feel like a helpless child. But I do not await a solution to my "problem." I may even say, as I sometimes do, "God, help me" or "God, give me strength." But I am not asking for a kind of infusion of heavenly assistance. I merely need to know that I am man and that He is God. Then I am ready to hurt, to feel pain, to see more clearly the artificial goals that helped to cause my pain. Then I am ready to pursue more honestly the genuine meaning of my life.

Similarly, I can accept the tension that is a part of my existence. I do not seek to assuage it with tranquilizers or to quiet it with alcohol. My tension is a revelation to me. It is a protest from my body and it tells me about the struggle of my spirit. It tells me that I am trying to be something that I am not, that I am afraid to be honest. I have somehow interrupted the flow of life; I have somehow, perhaps mysteriously and unaware, refused to face myself. I am seeking the approval that I must first give myself, or I am attempting to be other than I am destined to be. My tension is a message from my God. It is direct and unmistakable; it demands attention. I can ignore it, as I am often obliged to do, but ultimately I must face it and discover God in the meaning of my life. It tells me that I am pretending to know more than I do, to appear more than I am. It tells me that I am wanting in faith.

Some men tell me that without such tension they cannot work. I do not believe them. I feel that such tension is an

artificial impetus to accomplishment. It is an abuse of the
marvelous being that man is. It reflects his confusion and
artificial goals. It is an infallible directive asking man to face
the meaning of his life, to reflect upon it. It comes when he
is afraid to tell people the truth, or when he is using them for
personal gain. It comes when he is rushing to finish work
that he could enjoy at another time. It comes when he
permits himself to be in situations that he loathes, situations
that he could have avoided had he had the courage to be
honest, situations in which he is not yet able to be himself. It
comes when he is attempting to do too much, to quiet his
restlessness with activity. My tension tells me that I have not
yet arrived, that perhaps I never will. That in itself does not
seem to matter. All that matters is that I am doing the best I
can to understand this unmistakable message that bids me
to live in complete honesty.

And in such tension I find my God, even as I find Him in
the moods that intensify my loneliness and force me back
upon myself. I have learned at such times as these to go apart
and to feel again my oneness with the world. I want my
being to flow with the rhythm of the sea gull and the
heaving ocean. I want my heart to join with the pulse of
the wind and the motion of the trees. I want to know the
serenity I feel when I swim in the ocean and spy upon the
tiny schools of fish, the purple sea urchins, the lobsters under
rocks, the lurking eels, and the multicolored starfish. And
when I am apart, I begin to know such serenity and rhythm;
I am again in contact with my manhood.

I could not continue to live without these reflective moments when I look at my life and evaluate my place in it. As
a child, I used to hit stones with a small baseball bat by the
hour. I needed this solitude to be in touch with myself. And

as a man, I need it still; unstructured time, priceless time
when I do not work or rush or converse, when I am alone
with myself, when I realize that I am one being in touch
with one world, one man in special contact with his God.

And when my reflective times are past, and I am once
again in contact with war and poverty and those I love, I
usually come away a different man. I find that material
comforts do not mean as much, that my work is not as
important as I thought, that my friendships can become
richer and deeper and more real. Such moments and moods
are a priceless revelation from my God. Afterward, I can
never again be quite the same, not because some divine law
demands it, but because I see more clearly the true and
honest values of my life.

I am not sure that I can begin to put these values into
words. I can only say that I sense my unity with all of
creation, that I am an integral part of life. It is then that I
can look at my wife and know how truly beautiful she is. It is
then that I can touch her hand, and this means more than
the more exciting and passionate moments of love. It is then
that I most want my parents to understand, then that I most
want to reveal myself to my friends. It is then that I can taste
food and enjoy its flavor, then that I want to swim in the
ocean and feel the waves on my flesh. It is then that I can see
a Negro and know that I must help him to fight, then that I
can read of war and know that it is futile and mad. It is then
that I can see the sun shimmering against the sea and the
white water splashing on the rocks and rejoice in the reality
of my own life. It is then that I do not have to have any
purpose in life, that life is its own purpose, that I am a part
of an undying kind of creation. I do not turn to my God and
say, "thank you!" I just *am* and this is quite enough. It is

then that I can look at my world and watch the *birth of God*.

I know that whenever a man is finding meaning, wherever a man is helped from darkness and again finds beauty and joy in his life, God is being born. I do not have to call Him "God," for "God" is but a word. I do not have to describe Him or to reflect His mind. I do not have to praise Him or to determine His will. I do not have to picture Him as a white-haired patriarch or to put the words of Western civilization in His mouth. I do not have to reduce Him to a system or to place in careful categories the rules that men have offered in His name. It is enough that a man smiles, or enjoys his work, or is freed from slavery, or rejoices in the birth of his child. Then I know that God is being born because man has meaning in his life.

I see the birth of God in the old Italian couple who run a grocery store in my neighborhood. They do not speak of God or Jesus or salvation. This couple love each other and greet me with a kind word and a smile. They smile when I buy a half-pound of hamburger for some homemade chili when my wife is gone. The store is their home, their life, their community. They know almost everyone by name, or at least, by face. They charge more than a supermarket, but they give more. And when I leave the store, I somehow feel more human, more in touch with the realities of life, more a man. They work every day from nine till nine. They eat lunch and dinner together while they work. And when I say, "You work too hard," they answer, "This is where we are the happiest." And I believe them. They do not work at all; they spend the day serving their friends. Then they go home, have a glass of wine, and watch TV. Sometimes they play cards or reminisce. Then they go to bed. At times I sing a little when

I leave their store, not because I have been "saved," but because in the beauty of this vision of man, I sense in my life the birth of God.

It would be humorous to me if someone would tell this couple to go to church, to receive the sacraments, to confess their sins. They are already in touch with God because they are in touch with the meaning of life. It is enough for them to go to one another, to laugh and cry with their friends, to confess their weariness at the end of a day. And in their simple lives, I see the birth of God.

I see the birth of God in the stranger with whom I share a drink in a lonely city away from home. He is a salesman, thirtyish, handsome, and alone. He asks about my work and tells me that he sells plywood. He is recently divorced, has two children living with his wife, and believes that any reconciliation is impossible. He has dated a dozen different girls in the past two months, but is tired of the chase and wants to settle down. He glances at an attractive blonde who is sitting near us. He sighs, rubs his hand over his right eye, looks at me and says, "What does it all mean?" I answer that I'm not always sure. Guiltily he talks of church and childhood, saying the same things I have heard a thousand times before: "I'm not very religious; the church routine doesn't do much for me." He sips his drink and asks, "Do you believe in God?" "Yes," I answer, "in my own way." "I wish I could," he says, "I've been looking for something all of my life."

I like him; he is honest and real and searching. Maybe for a time he has to wander around to lose the sense of failure that comes from his unhappy marriage. But he is absorbed with the question of meaning, and that, to me, is the question of God. He wants to know if life leads anywhere. So for a pair of drinks we reveal a bit of ourselves and then walk anonymously away. I am more at home with him than with the prophets of religion who speak of "sin" and "redemption." I am in touch with a human being who is searching for a God as real as a martini, as fulfilling as the genuine love of a woman, as tangible as the personal exchange of words between friends. And in the reality of his search, I feel the birth of God.

I have a close friend who rejects the very notion of God. Yet he is as "religious" as any man I know. His feelings about God may well reflect the hypocrisy and ignorance he discovered in the Fundamentalist faith of his childhood. Or, it may be the result of his own mature experience. I do not know. But I know that he is trying to make his life mean something. He has no time for God the magician, or the God Who turns men's attention away from life. He only has time for the friends who need him, the students he teaches, the work he loves. He has refused several jobs that pay more money but do not mean as much as the job he has. He is sensitive, compassionate, strong, and utterly honest. His children are warm and curious, happy and alive. He takes life as it comes, requires no assurance of an afterlife, can be loyal to his wife without the command of a lawgiver, can live simply without the vows of a monk. He has no time for churches, nor have they time for him. Those who would call him an atheist reveal how little they know of God. For the God in whom I profess faith is not different from the sacred concern my friend has for the meaning of life.

I would not live differently if I suddenly recognized that my faith in God were an illusion. Nor would my friend change his way of life if he became aware of a living God. Neither of us is loyal to some way of life that contradicts the inner longing of our own spirit. We do not try to be honest

because God has requested it, but because it is the only way
we can life comfortably with ourselves. In reality, I do not
differ "religiously" from my friend. I do not try to convert
him. I listen to him, enjoy him, love him. And in his
honesty, I know the birth of God.

My God is alive and mysterious. He does not terrorize me
with His laws and punishments, nor does He bore me with
His dull prayers and empty rituals. He does not harangue me
about my weakness, but teaches me to grow in strength. He
does not call me an unworthy son since He has fashioned me
through the miracle of millions of years of growth and
change. He teaches me to smile at my failures, to try again,
to do the best I can. He does not reproach me for my
weakness, but teaches me that my very weakness and need is
the reason that I can be loved. He does not want me to be
perfect, only to be honest and alive. He does not want me to
live in fear of Him or to be saturated with guilt; He wants
my freedom. He does not limit His messages to sacred books,
nor does He share His powers with special consecrated
persons. He does not communicate in special sects. He
speaks to me in the wind and the rain, in the curiosity of a
child, in the touch of a friend's hand, in the look of one I
love.

He is in the water before it is blessed, in the bread and
wine before priests pray over it and turn it to myth. I do not
speak to Him in intimate conversations or in special prayers.
I do not have to speak to Him at all. I am aware of Him, and
that is enough. He is most present to me when I am most
present to myself, when I am most present and real to other
men. He is at the depths of my very own being. I cannot
define Him or reduce Him to rules. I cannot fathom His
mind or the mystery of His joy. When I think about Him, I
am more apt to smile than to frown.

Learned men ask me if He is transcendent or immanent, which means is He something more than I am, or a mere extension and projection of myself? I do not know how to answer them. I am not sure that I understand their words, or if I do understand, I am not sure that I can answer them. Somehow the question doesn't seem important. I don't know how it can be solved. I can only say that at times He seems to be other than I am, at other times He is so much a part of my own existence that to talk to Him would be like talking to myself. I must leave such speculations to minds that are more differently attuned than mine, since I do not see the possibility or the importance of a solution.

I cannot speak of God as though I am speaking of some exceptional human person. Nor can I picture Him thus. To speak of God's personality or variety of personalities is to create an amalgam of sterile words. The ancient Jews did well not to mention His name. I cannot fathom God; I can only describe my feeble experience of Him and assert that He gives meaning to my life. I can attempt more, but it would not be real for me. Neither is it real for me to ask God for favors. This reduces God to a comfortable religious myth and permits men to make up rules according to which God is controlled.

And now, in my search for God, I can appreciate Jesus Christ. I do not look to him for salvation; I do not pray to him. I do not beg him to do what I must do myself. He does not mystify me with his words. He does not make love complicated or turn it into a definition. He is not a theologian, but a brother; not a preacher, but a friend. He can get the attention of a man in a bar, a prostitute, a laborer, or a millionaire. He speaks of the hungry, the sick, the prisoners, the sad, and he asks man to give them help.

But most of all, he tells every man that he counts in the

sight of God. He tells him this by the attention he gives, by the time he spends, by the patience he has. He has no program, no routine. He goes about doing good, knowing well that he cannot live long enough to do all of it, but knowing equally well that he can do some of it. He announces the birth of God in his love for men, in his effort to wipe out the distinction between Jew and gentile, slave and free, even man and woman, and to see every man as good.

This is the Jesus I know. I do not recognize the marble monuments in which frightened men have buried him. Nor do I believe the doting mother-churches that brag that he belongs exclusively to them. Nor do I accept easily the arrogance of men who ask me if Jesus is my Saviour, and who leave me cold when they tell me he is theirs. Such men look at me with hardly human eyes. The Jesus I know is not saved. He is in a rage to love men. He looks *at* man, not *through* him. He is a friend. No friend of mine looks at me and asks with self-satisfied pride: "Are you saved?" If he cares one whit, he talks to me, not as a salvation-monger, but as a man. Then somehow he is like Jesus, even if he has never heard his name. Then somehow, like Jesus, he tells me of the birth of God.

My God is not dead, the whole world speaks of Him and tells me of His birth. The Negroes' struggle for freedom is the relentless voice of God. Once the Negro knew another kind of God and was content to sing mournful hymns and to hang his head. Once he prayed to a white God Who told him to tolerate his slavery and bow to his master in a timid and broken spirit. Now I see the wrath of the true and living God Who marches in Washington and rages in Detroit. I see the birth of God in the black man's determination to work and eat and send his children to a decent school. I see

God in the fire of dark eyes and in the courage of a strong mouth with full lips. I see the birth of God in slums and speeches, in the fight for open housing, and in the strength of brave men who are ready to go to jail. I see the birth of God because the Negro is demanding a meaningful life in place of slavery.

I see God's birth in the struggle to end poverty and in the protests that hope to end war. I see His birth in the hearts of men who wince with every bullet, who shudder at napalm, and who detest every bomb. I see Him born in the screams of the children who do not understand the gunfire that keeps them from playing. I see Him born in the mothers who will not give their sons to war and violence, in the young women who will not watch their husbands die in vain. I see Him born in the philosophers who insist that the freedom purchased by war is not freedom at all if a child or a spouse is murdered, if a home and family are destroyed.

I see the birth of God in the comedian who makes me laugh, in the young man who interviews me with trembling lips, in the joy of the World Series, in the excitement of a no-hitter, in a young pitcher's struggle to win thirty games. I see the birth of God in a heart transplant, in the excitement of the Preakness or the Kentucky Derby, in a child's attempt to walk, in a baby's struggle to say a meaningful word. I see the birth of God in a work of art that makes me gasp, in a piece of sculpture that tells me something of myself. I see the birth of God in the whole school of art that reaches beyond the obvious, that insists on more than photographing or rendering, that touches the secrets of existence. I see it in the colors and forms, the shades and contrasts that insist that life is delicate and refined, indescribable and tenuous, bold and exciting. I see God's birth in an old man's refusal to die, in his determination to endure the operation that may save his life. I see it in a young man's dream, in an adolescent's turmoil. I see the birth of God wherever man is searching for meaning, wherever life is struggling to express itself, wherever hands are reaching out to grasp other hands, where strong hearts whisper to weak ones: "You can."

I see God's birth in the men who explore the sea to feed the future nations, in the scientists who struggle to regulate a world's population, in the scientists who purify the air so men can breathe. I see it in the fight for mental health, in the experiments for better education, in the new forms of communication, in the effort to improve a program of Medicare. I see God's birth in the welfare worker who brings help to the poor amid frustration and ingratitude and red tape. I see it in the teachers in the slums, in the men and women of Vista and the Peace Corps, in new housing, in any effort to give men hope and to make their lives mean something.

I do not agree with the prophets of doom who maintain that morality is at an end, who deplore the sexual irresponsibility of our age, who assert that modern man wants freedom without discipline. I do not agree with the surpliced leaders who plead with men to return to the churches, who refurbish their empty ceremonies and reword their archaic sermons to keep men captive in their religious institutions. God is not in the churches, and He is not in the legends and myths that frightened and resentful men have fashioned. God is in the struggle of honest men to be themselves, in the effort of brave men to care, in the courage of weak men to do the best they can, in the determination of leaders in the global village to provide men with the love and equality that is their due.

God is not dead. The churches are. God is not dead. The religious sects are. God lives and is born in man's effort to be fulfilled and free. Outside my window I can see a little boy at play. He is bouncing a tennis ball against a brick wall, and he may be playing "baseball" like I used to do. I hope he never feels, as I once did, that he has to confess his sins, that he has to appease an angry God, that he has to be rescued or redeemed. I hope that he will make every day mean something, that he will be open and honest enough to have a friend, that his parents will love him and permit him to be free. I hope that he will care about other men, regardless of their race or religion, that he will be free enough to search for meaning and for God. I hope that he will not have to fight in Vietnam or anywhere else, that he will have time to grow and love and care about the poor. I hope that he will be satisfied to do the best he can and to know that no matter what he does or doesn't do, he counts. I hope he can find meaning amid loneliness, purpose amid discouragement and failure, love in the midst of his search. I hope he knows that in his struggle to be himself, in his effort to find himself in the global village, he is assisting in the *birth of God.*